A CHICANO SPANISH TEACHER

by

Sonny Morín

Copyright © 2023 by Sonny Morin.

ISBN 978-1-956691-11-5 (hardcover)
ISBN 978-1-956691-12-2 (ebook)
Library of Congress Control Number: 2023902222

All rights reserved. No part of this book may be reproduced or transmitted in any form or by any means, electronic or mechanical, including photocopying, recording, or by any information storage and retrieval system without express written permission from the author, except in the case of brief quotations embodied in critical reviews and certain other noncommercial uses permitted by copyright law.

This book is a work of fiction. Names, characters, places, and incidents are the product of the author's imagination or are used fictitiously. Any resemblance to actual locales, events, or persons, living or dead, is purely coincidental.
Printed in the United States of America.

OrionPress
www.orionpressbooks.com
1382 Belmont Road, Raymond, WA 98577

To My Ancestors
&
For My Family

Special Thanks to
Clorinda and Carlos Torres
And Graciela Peña for your friendship and support

CONTENTS

1. Origins..3
2. Glory Days 15
3. Higher Education..25
4. Graduate School..46
5. Public Schools 62
6. Junior High..79
7. Teaching in Alaska 88
8. Full Circle 120
9. A Homecoming?..130
10. Final Assignment...146
11. Changes 159
12. Onward Through the Fog.................................175
13. Acknowledgements:..179

Preface

I never started out wanting to be a teacher, especially not a Spanish teacher. I remember telling someone in my high school class, "Who would ever want to be a Spanish teacher? Definitely not me and here we are. I started doing what I thought was pretty easy and they were going to pay me on top of that! These are stories that give you some background cultural information growing up as a Chicano. I'll talk about my aspirations, my early educational opportunities and making it through graduate school as a teacher. Teaching opened up opportunities to travel and meet all kinds of people. I'll give credit to all those who helped me along the way and in return, I will always try to do the same. Seeing my father work as hard as he did made me want to work that way as well. As a public school teacher, you get to see all kinds of things. I'm glad that I had a psychology background to help me maneuver in some of those situations. I always told myself that I would stop teaching when it wasn't fun anymore. And by the way, I did reach that point. I worked with some of the best people that I have ever met. Some teachers have quite a bit to offer their students. I strived to better myself so that I could be a better teacher to my students. I tried to emulate the excellent teachers that I had. I learned that you cannot jump to conclusions. It's better to get the students to want to come to class because they trust you and enjoy being in my class. It should not be an, "us against them attitude," but a, hey I'm just here to help you where I can. I will tell you about some of these experiences that span just over thirty years.

1. Origins

It was a cold December night when I came into this world. I came home with my mother, Clorinda, who lived with her parents Mamo and Papo, at home. My father, Tino, was in Germany, serving in the U.S. Army. I didn't see him until I was three! I'll get to that later. Once home from the hospital, after about a week or so friends, family and neighbors came to see the "new" baby, me!

One day after the next-door neighbor Joey, stopped by, I began to develop a high fever. They took me to the Dr., but he couldn't find any reason for the fever. The fever kept getting higher and everyone was panicking, then my grandmother remembered Joey was the last one to see me. She told someone to quickly get a hold of him. They did and he came by, my grandmother told him to touch me and with that the fever broke! She said that he had given me "ojo." Frequently called the "evil eye," it is better called "strong vision." It's like an admiration of something or someone and jinxing it in some way. My grandfather was guilty of having that. My Mamo made sure Papo would touch any little kid he met. It was just a little pat and a rub on the head and forehead to prevent them from getting ill. I grew up with all of these folkloric illnesses, afflictions and superstitions. Doctors can't cure everything and science can't explain everything either.

That being said, I grew up having "barridas," being swept with a broom, and "curado de susto," which means "cured of fright" by being rubbed with an egg. If I had an accident or some kind of incident that scared me, or that was traumatic got me one of the two. The "barrida" seems to re-energize the aura, the human energy field. I have also read somewhere that eggs have a "drawing" kind of property, sucking out the negativity. That was used if they thought someone had given me "ojo."

A little information about my grandparents, I called them Mamo and Papo because I couldn't pronounce grandma nor grandpa. My grandfather, Papo, as I was told, used to hide behind his house smoking cigarettes when he was five years old. He could not read nor write, albeit he could write his name in cursive, something many kids don't know how to do these days. Anyway, he was an auto mechanic and could fix anything. My bicycle handle bars broke off and he took it to work and brought it back good to go! He could barely speak English, but he could still communicate with the gringos when he had to. He had no problem communicating. Sometimes my grandmother, Mamo would send him to the store and would write symbols for him to get whatever they needed. He would always tell me to walk the "straight road, el camino derecho mijo" he would say. I remember the time I really pissed him off. He had given me a grinder with a wire brush wheel. I took it and brought it back since it didn't work. It wouldn't turn on. I told him, "Papo, no quiero yonke!" Oh shit! He took it from me and threw it down. I kind of laughed a little. He gave me another one that did work, and for many years at that!

Papo had made it through most of his life before he went to see a medical Dr. He had a hernia for a long time and used to use a hernia belt. My mother finally talked him into getting it fixed. He must have been in his seventies and I was in my twenties. He was to stay overnight in the hospital and was a little nervous. I told him that I would stay with him and I did. He was very brave and so very polite to everyone and they loved him for it! We took a walk outside the hospital on the sidewalk and shared a *Swisher Sweet* cigar, not the same one!

My Mamo was one of many brothers and a sister growing up in the ranches of South Texas around Duval County. She only had an eighth-grade education, but she was so smart, she was "al alva" like we say. She had it going on. She was a reader and did pay attention to politics as well. I guess that's where I get my interest of both of those things. She used to go and pick up people who couldn't get to the polls.

My mother told me that she would often drag her to these political gatherings, trying to get people to vote. She was a strong woman growing up with a bunch of brothers. She dropped out of school so that her little brother my uncle Bert could be the first to graduate from high school. I had many great-uncles who always came by to visit her and us. She grew up a Gonzalez, and let me tell you, it's an extremely large family. I believe she had ten brothers and a sister and from those came hundreds. When all of the brothers were still alive we began to have family reunions, huge gatherings with so much food, and it was so great to see all of my cousins and their families. We began having them once a year, but that was too much. There were so many people. We then had them every so often five or ten years. After my uncle Bert died his daughter, Marie and my mother organized what was our most recent reunion back in 2018. We all paid for our own meal and met in San Antonio at the Little Red Barn. I'm not sure when we will have another one. I guess it's the younger generation's turn to pick up the torch.

 I also want to mention a little bit about my maternal great-grandmother, "Granny" as my mother and all of her grandchildren called her. She apparently, had an excellent sense of humor. I would like to think that I may have inherited some of that as well. She loved to laugh and was always laughing. My mother told me about the time that she and Granny after they listened on the radio to their "novellas" Granny had gone to sit in the rocking chair and was rocking quite hard. Well, the rocking chair leg had been broken, and she fell off of the chair and fell right into the closet. My mother could hear her laughing in the closet! How funny! When Granny would go and visit my relatives, her children in George West, she would sleep with the girls, her grand-daughters, in their room. She would have them all cracking up laughing. My uncle Joe would come in and yell at them, "¡Ya duérmanse!" Go to sleep already! Granny would then mock him, her son, as he was walking away and would have them all cracking up all over again! I wish I had gotten to know her in this world. I'm sure she's looking out for all of us and I know I'll see her one day.

My paternal grandmother, Mama Lola, died when I was very young, about six years old. I found out through Ancestry.com that she was from Puerto Rico. I don't know very much about her, only that she wanted to bury my umbilical cord after it had fallen off, as my mother had told me. Also, that she came to Alice for three weeks to help her after I was born. She said that Mama Lola would hand wash all of my diapers and would hang them out to dry then bring them in and iron them all! This is before there were any disposable diapers. My mother told her that she didn't have to do that. She would tell her, "no quiero que se resfrie" I don't want him to get cold. She also made the best fried chicken. I also think that I inherited my vision problems from her. She as I recently found out, was completely blind as a young adult. She later regained some vision but had to use coke-bottle thick glasses to help her see. When she read, she would hold whatever she was reading right up to her eye to see the words.

My grandfather, Papa Marcos and she lived in Orange Grove, a small town about twenty miles from Alice. My grandfather was born in 1888! One of our families had a picture with him and Pancho Villa on horseback, but I don't know if he rode with Villa or not. I wish I could have seen it! He grew up near Rio Grande City on the Texas-Mexico border.

I was told that he had an accident where he had fallen off of his horse. He had gone to the medical doctors and they told him that he would never walk again. Not satisfied, he went to see a very famous curandero, Don Pedrito Jaramillo. He was based near Falfurrias, Texas. I remember reading about his remedies in my Chicano Literature class at the university. Well, he did indeed walk again. I think that he was given some kind of special water to rub on his legs. For all of Don Pedrito's remedies you had to do it "sin vergüenza," "without shame." Papa Marcos lived to be 96 years old. He had cancer of the larynx and had to have it removed. He couldn't speak so I learned to read lips in Spanish! My mother was very good at it. We would go and visit him at the nursing home. He was always doing for others. He had planted flowers all around the nursing home where he was at.

He liked walking the halls with me at his side. He would motion to everyone that I was one of his grandchildren, he was so happy. I wish that we as a society would take better care of our elderly population by helping their caregivers who are not helped any more than what they should. It's such a shame in our culture the way we treat our elderly in their so-called "golden years."

Going back to Ancestry.com, it turned out that I was twenty-two percent Greek, twenty-two percent Italian, twenty-two percent Iberian Peninsula, these are on my mother's side of the family, Hinojosa – Gonzalez; Thirty-three percent Native American (Northern Mexico) on my father's side, Morín – Bentancourt.

My grandmother Mamo raised me on medicinal teas, such as yerbabuena, alucema, toronjil and té de limón. She grabbed some herbs out of her backyard or would tell me to get them. She had a tea for everything and would boil up some leaves and pour me a cup. One day I was out playing by myself pretending that I was "Freddy the Freeloader" from the Red Skelton Show. Freddy always had a jug of XXX brew. So, I grabbed what I thought was an empty bottle of bleach. I opened it and took a swig. I swallowed what little there was in it. Oh my! I ran into the house and they started giving me all kinds of stuff to drink like water, Coca Cola and other stuff.

My grandmother also had one of those old tub washers with two rollers on top that would wring out the excess water. She was doing a load and the rollers were rolling. I was fascinated, maybe even a little mesmerized. I wondered, "What if I... AHHHHHHH! My arm got sucked in up to my shoulder! Good thing my grandfather was out back to get my arm out. I guess I'm a stubborn learner or just retarded but, I went back and looked at the rollers again and thought, "What if I...AHHHHHH! No fucking shit! I did it again. What a moron! Since I'm on the subject of my f'ups, when we moved to the new house on Dewey St. I took another fascination with red ants. I sat down, yes, twice on a red ant nest. I literally had ants in my pants! I must have had my parents a little worried.

Growing up Catholic, belief in God was also important. I remember being a little kid in church and realizing that Jesus had died on the cross. I was so upset and crying, stretched out on the pew. My mother would later drag me to church on Dec. 12 for the Day of the Virgin of Guadalupe which was also my birthday. I feel lucky that she is my patron saint.

My grandmother had a prayer for everything. She told me to make sure that I pray to God first, because he was a jealous God. Only then I could call on the saints for their help. There's a saint for every occasion. When you lose something, say a little prayer to God then ask St. Anthony for help. Leave it at that and let them do their work! For a lost cause, pray to St. Jude and of course to La Virgén de Guadalupe, my patron saint. The way it was explained to me is that the saints, being saints, have a stronger signal to God than we do and they can act on our behalf. They sort of boost our signal to God. I believe in the power of prayer. It has always worked for me, "¡Dios es muy grande!" I don't push my beliefs on anyone and at this point in my life really don't care what someone may or may not think.

I graduated through the Catholic Church when I was a senior in high school. Growing up Catholic, I believe in good over evil and that there is a God. My views aren't dogmatic like the Church's. On abortion all I'm going to say is that if you are against abortion, don't have one, period. If this doesn't apply to you, then sit down and shut the fuck up! I believe in kindness, honesty and hard work among other things. When people call themselves Christian, I think, *"What?" "Already?"* It's an everyday thing, to try and be Christian-like and be a good person. People can call themselves anything they want, but it doesn't mean a thing. These right-wingers who call themselves "Christians" are anything but. They are the opposite. They sure could learn better from the Atheists, who are more Christian-like than they themselves!

Growing up I understood Spanish more than I spoke it. I could speak it in a rudimentary manner to get my point across. Most of my friends in the neighborhood were the same way. Some of my other friends from school may have spoken more. We weren't even allowed to speak Spanish when I was in elementary school. It was prohibited. What a bunch of fucking racist morons! Now we know that children can learn more than one language at a time!

My father, Tino as he was called, returned home from overseas. I was three years old. I can remember going to the airport to pick him up in San Antonio. Once home in Alice, I didn't know who he was and did not want him near my mother. I would try to kick him off of the bed. I eventually got used to him. My parents had saved enough money to move out of my grandparents' and get a home of their own. It was a typical neighborhood in Alice, Texas. My father used to work for Knolle Farms, as an ice cream salesman. He drove a yellow truck. When he was in his early 30's he had a heart attack. My Godfather, Luis came to pick me up after school. I knew something was up. He took me to the hospital and I saw my father through the window in the door and he had all these tubes connected to him. He had a heart attack. He would not go back to that job, but go to college for diesel mechanics. He got his Associates Degree as a Master Mechanic and did that until he retired. He traveled all over the U.S. fixing engines and compressors in malls, factories and plants. He worked very hard and I was always so proud of him. People everywhere knew him. I remember being a kid and we were in some place in the middle of nowhere and I would hear someone say, "Hey Tino!" When my brother Adrian went and worked with him up north, the same thing. They'd be in some isolated location somewhere in Minnesota or Iowa and he would hear someone call out, "Hey Tino!"

My grandparents really had a huge influence on me. I started Kindergarten at four years old. My mother didn't want me to sit out a whole year. She enrolled me in the Kindergarten at the Episcopal Church. I also attended private first grade school. When we moved out of my grandmother's, I attended public school for the first time.

In those days school was brutal, I mean some teachers were mean and cruel. I remember my fourth-grade teacher, Miss Flowers. Oh my! She was scary. She wouldn't let us go to the bathroom when we needed to. Everyone, and I mean everyone, wet themselves, boys and girls. No one ever laughed, ever. It was so humiliating. I swore that if I was ever a teacher, I wouldn't treat kids that way. Then in the fifth grade my teacher, Mr. Godines had to leave the class for a moment and told us to stay in our seats. Well, we sat in groups, and José decided to get out of his chair and squat down bouncing a nerf ball on the wall. All of a sudden, the teacher walks in! Oh snap! He told José to come up in front of the class and he took out his paddle and gave him a swat. We were scared shitless! No one said a word. How freaking barbaric our educational system used to be, and in some ways still is. Here was a big man hitting on a little fifth grader? That is f'd up! In sixth grade I was in my geography class sitting behind my friend Adam. Our teacher Mr. Gomez told the class to be quiet and settle down. Adam sitting in the very front, turned around and yelled at the class, YEAH! Mr. Gomez turned around and looked at him with some "crazy eyes." He was a former marine, and he walks over to Adam and grabs him by the arm and shakes him out of his desk and onto the floor like a rag doll! If Adam's dad would have been there I don't think he would have done that. Mr. Gomez then takes him out into the hallway and gives him a swat. These days many of those actions would be considered criminal acts and he would very likely and rightly get sued and or jailed! However, that compared to have to face a "live shooter" with an assault rifle walking the hallways looking to kill anyone, well, there's no comparison is there?

    The way it was at home for me and many of my friends, if we got in trouble at school, then we would get in way worse trouble at home. So, like a normal person, I tried to avoid getting in trouble. I still did. I got a swat in seventh grade for chewing gum. I had a pair of thick burgundy corduroy pants and didn't feel it. But when I got three swats in Jr. High from Mr. Cadena, Oh shit. Those did hurt. We got caught skipping school after my mother let Adam and I sleep in after my first concert, The Doobie Brothers. We were supposed to go back at lunch, but drove around town and school. What dumbasses! The principal said he could call my mom and suspend me, or take three licks. I said, give me the licks. She still found out and I couldn't go to concerts for two years! Oh well, "what you gonna do?" When I went to English class first period after the swats Mr. Cadena had given me, I sat down in my seat and Oh! I couldn't sit down! It hurt so f'ing much! It took about fifteen minutes to subside, little by little putting all of my weight down.

When I got to high school, it was easier to skip class. The class rosters were printed on card stock paper with perforations to easily tear off the attendance for each day. The teacher would circle in pencil the "A" for absent or "T" for tardy, by the names of those students who were either. The office would then send student workers to pick up the slips on a clip outside of the classroom door. Well, I knew the students who would pick up the slips and would get them to erase my circled "A" for absent. I did this my entire sophomore and first half of my junior year in high school.

One morning in the Spring of my junior year, I was about to enter the gym just before 7:00 a.m., when I see one of the other quarterbacks just drive up. I don't know what got into me, but before he could get out of his car, I went over and told him that we should just blow off practice. He needed no convincing, so I got in his car and we took off. We just drove around smoking weed. As QB's we had to show up an hour early to do all of our QB workouts, before the rest of the team showed up at 8:00. On our cruise we saw another friend who was dropping off his brother at an elementary school. We pulled up to the stop sign, and the other friend plows his car into our vehicle. He didn't see us stop. Crap!

We managed to unstick the cars and head back to school. As I was walking to my locker, I saw my Head Coach standing there with the attendance form in his hand. *Oh shit!* I thought. He quietly told me not to go to baseball practice, but to go to straight to his office. The assistant principal called me to his office. I told him that I had permission not to be there. So, he picked up the phone and called my mother. Oh snap! I got on the phone with her and said, "You remember when I told you that..." and she straight up told me, "Mijo, I'm not going to lie for you!" That was it. I looked at the principal and told him that I wouldn't do it anymore and he let me leave without any repercussions from the school or my parents. I got lucky. I still had to talk to the coach. It was agony all day knowing that I would have to. I go into his office and told him that I wouldn't do it again. He too let me go, so I went on to baseball practice and it was over and done with. I never did skip school again. My other two friends spent a couple of hours with the coach.

My parents were strict, but loving, and once I learned how to play the game, they gave me a lot of freedom. My best friend J.A. taught me how to drive when I was twelve, he was probably fourteen. My dad already had a few cold ones. That was the best time to ask him for anything.

Confession: I learned to drive a standard four on the floor stick shift in a red VW bug. I drove it everywhere. On my last day of Junior-High I drove it to school and parked in the back behind the field house. When I took Driver's Ed. as a sophomore, I had to drive myself to class. I would park at the very end of the parking lot and crouch down as I walked to the campus. After one of my Little League baseball games at night, my dad let me drive to the beach in Corpus. We often stayed at Dr. Joseph's condo. It was dark and here I was twelve years old driving down farm road 665, hauling ass at 75 mph, the backway to Corpus, trying to keep up with my mother!

Confession: I was thirteen when I smoked my first joint. It would have been the summer after I learned to drive. I didn't even believe it was real. So we smoked it all. My buddy was right behind me and I thought he had disappeared! I start to call out for him and he says "I'm right here next to you." I told him that I was going to go to bed before my parents got home. I was so stoned on commercial weed, now called "reggie" or "schwag." I was such a square before J.A. introduced me to weed and music other than the Beatles. He gave me his brother's Black Sabbath Paranoid to take home and listen. From then on, I listened to every band popular at the time, and there were many.

A CHICANO SPANISH TEACHER

In the Spring of 1976, I was fifteen years old. I had already been ungrounded from going to concerts and had been to see Rush on their "All The World's A Stage" tour the previous Fall. I was a big fan of the band Moxy, a Canadian band. They were very popular in the Seventies in San Antonio and south Texas. They were going to be playing in Corpus Christi at the Ritz Theater. My best friend Pooh gets permission from his parents. He's only twelve or thirteen, but his parents trust me and by now, have earned my parents trust as well. We head on out in my red VW bug. We get there and pay $5.25 for the ticket. The opening band was a band on their first U.S. Tour. It was an Australian band call AC/DC. They opened up. OMG! They freaking rocked the show. They were promoting their "Let There Be Rock" album. I got an AC/DC t-shirt for $5.00!

Music is still very important to me. Although my parents did enjoy music it was Tejano or Mexican music. I liked rock and roll!

Our town of Alice in the 60's and 70's was about fifty-fifty, white and Hispanic, with a few blacks sprinkled in. It was still a little racist. It wasn't as overt as it is now in 2021. The railroad tracks separated the town. You know the saying, "he or she lives on the other side of the tracks." I knew I'd be going to college. I was going to play baseball. I could get into any state college or university having graduated in the top ten percent of my class. "No Affirmative Action," needed, thank you very much! I had bought into the macho BS of sports and coaches, always practicing something, I did not really know or think about what I was going to study in college. I spent most of my time playing sports and chasing girls. Not much time for anything else, except maybe a concert. It was like the old saying goes, sex, drugs, and rock n roll! It was like, *Fast Times at Ridgemont High, Dazed and Confused and Rock City* all rolled into one.

All in all, I was very lucky growing up, especially in the Dewey neighborhood. We had woods in the back behind the alley. My friends and I always made camps or treehouses there. It was such an innocent time compared to nowadays. Alice was a little oil boom town, lots of drilling companies. Many of my friends went to work after high school on the oil rigs and when I would see them, they would have a roll of money, like three thousand dollars or more. I barely had three dollars! They were buying houses and cars, but then when the oil market crashed in the 80's, many lost everything. Alice was like a ghost town. Many people started moving away. I didn't think that I would be back. Family changes everything! After leaving at seventeen years old, I would be returning some twenty-six years later at forty-three years old. That story will come later in the book.

2. Glory Days

As I mentioned earlier, I had some success as an athlete growing up which I believe gave me the confidence to succeed in other aspects of my life. Sports taught me how to persevere and be innovative to adapt to a situation or solve whatever issue may arise either on or off the field. I found success first in baseball.

Baseball

My uncle Jorge started me with a stick and chinaberries to hit like a baseball. He started working with me when I was three years old. That's all we did for several years. It was so much fun and I was good at it. By the time I was seven years old I was able to be a bat boy. The kids in our neighborhood were mostly all on the same team, so I would be the bat boy that first year. At practice I kept asking the coach to let me bat against any pitcher, but he never did let me. What the hell? He thought, I guess that I would get hurt. Oh please! I was so disappointed. I couldn't wait for next year when I could actually play.

That first game I played second base. They hit a grounder to me so I went to field it and the ball rolled up my glove and arm and hit me in the chin! I did pick up the ball and threw it, but I believe he was safe. The ball was so white and new and the lights so bright at night. It was almost like being in a dream. You had to be nine years old to make the All-Star team, but we had a player that was so good and only eight years old that did make the All-Star team. We would later play high school baseball and he would be my college roommate for one semester!

I went on and made the All-Star team the following years and at practice, which was at one o'clock with the sun high in the sky. The coach hit a fly ball to me that was very high. Well, the sun got in my eye and the ball hit me below my left eye and it knocked me out. The next thing I knew I was at the school by the practice field and the coach had carried me to the water faucet to put some water on my face. I told the coach, who was also a DPS patrolman, my mother worked at a Dr's office down the street. He took me and the Dr. told me that I would not be able to play in the All-Star game, and I couldn't believe it and started to cry. He was only joking, thank God! I did appreciate his humor though. This was my first eye trauma, there would be more throughout the years.

I would get much better in Little League. I was drafted by the Heldt Bros. team and was ten and the older players were twelve years old. We would win the City Championship that year and then again two years later when I was twelve. I did make the All-Star team at eleven years old. I hadn't hit a homerun yet, but my friend Vince, hit about eight or nine that year. He was amazing! We would also be college roommates for a couple of years in Brownsville. That boy had some potential.

The best coaching tip that I ever got was in Little League and it was to raise my back elbow while at bat. After that I started making unbelievable contact. That first game, at my first at bat, I hit the ball so hard, it was just getting momentum as it flew over the fence! The coach said that it would have gone out of the big field at Anderson Park. Once you find that sweet part of the bat, it's all over. On my third at bat that first game, I hit one out that broke one of the lights in the outfield. Everyone in the line-up hit homeruns. We also had the best pitcher in the league. He threw so freaking hard! Often he would throw nine pitches, it was like 1-2-3 you're out, three times!

We beat the other All-Star team in town and we played Falfurrias next. They had a curveball pitcher who was supposed to be pretty good. When a right-hander throws a curve to a left-handed hitter, the ball breaks perfectly right where I like it. I popped up the first time, but then homered twice after that. We lost by one run! The coach told me years later that they wanted to be fair and let everyone play. So, they let another catcher catch for Vince, and he could not handle hit pitching like our usual catcher. That Falfurrias team went pretty far, I think they almost made the Little League World Series. We could have been there! Oh well, what you gonna do? Remember Rule #1 Win the game first!

I went on to play Senior League and Big League along with playing all through high school. I thought that we would win district my senior year in high school, but sadly we came out in last place, unlike football. Our team did lead our district in homeruns however. I did make the All-District First Team as an outfielder my senior year. I did hit three homeruns that year, two in a game against Robstown.

I would later play with a player from that Little League Falfurrias team in a Big League All-Star tournament in San Antonio. In a game during that tournament we played what would be the longest that I would play, seventeen innings! In about the fifteenth inning they hit a grounder to me in shallow right-field. There was a runner on second. The runner was going for it. I couldn't believe it since it was an easy shot. So, I gunned it to the catcher Rob from Robstown. It was a perfect throw way before the runner got to home plate. Rob braced himself for a blow. The runner tried to make him drop the ball as he plowed into Rob. The runner was out. The next inning there was another runner on second base. This time they hit a shot between center field and left. The centerfielder had to run and field the ball, then make the throw to home. I thought, that was it, game over. It would have to be a perfect throw. As I'm running towards the dugout he freaking makes the throw! Same thing, Rob got plowed again. Now, he was a small guy, but tough dude!

I did give it a try in college at Hill Junior College and Texas Southmost College without too much success. I did have a good run at it though! The All-Star I mentioned earlier and another player from Falfurrias would also later be two of my college roommates in

Brownsville. Vince was the only real contender for pro ball, but we all gave it a shot!

After Big League all there was left was Semi-Pro baseball. Alice had a team called the "Mohawks." I hit my only grand-slam homer against Falfurrias at their field. It was over the center field fence which was at 410 feet! I didn't even know that the bases were loaded. I thought that there were only two people on base. I also played for the "Rebels" of San Marcos one summer while in college. I got some good playing time until the off-season pros came on the team. This would be my last attempt at playing ball.

I thought about trying out for the SWTSU baseball team, but it was only a club back in the early 80's, and you had to pay your own way! No thanks!

Football

In my hometown at the time, Junior High was eighth and ninth grade, and high school was tenth through twelfth grade. Most kids surrounding area schools started playing in seventh grade. My small group of friends and myself went out for football. I played tight end and it was really tough making it through the whole season. Our very first scrimmage on the kickoff, I was running down the field, staying in my lane while looking for the ball when all of a sudden someone on the other team came and "ear-holed" me so freaking hard that when I hit the ground I couldn't not believe what I was doing there. I was also on the kickoff return team. I wasn't the deep back, but the next one up. I was on the right side of the field when they kicked off to us and the ball was coming straight to me! I thought, *Oh no, oh no, oh no!* I did catch it and ran about five yards and got hammered. I wasn't sure if I would finish the season and it just started!

We lost one game by 40 points and the following day the coach made us run 40 wind-sprints. Our practice field was full of stickers and ants and that did not matter one bit. We all got stickers and ant bites.

A CHICANO SPANISH TEACHER

My friends and I all said to each other, "If you quit, I'll quit too." None of us ever did quit. We never won a game but tied two games and it was as if we had won a championship! My good friend was the QB, Donny, and another friend was a split end. Our best play was 48 Power Bootleg Pass. We scored most of our touchdowns on that play. Oh, I never caught a pass, but did drop a couple.

There was a new coach the following year and they wanted to do their own evaluations. So we all ran 40 yard dashes and threw the football and punted and kicked. They assigned me to the QB position. There would be two teams, the Orange and the White. I was on the White. At first, everyone at practice had different color jerseys. We would practice against each other. I was on the blue team and the last string quarterback. I kept moving up until I took the last string team and scored with them. I became the first stringer.

Coach Cruz was a small man. He did not look like a football Coach, but that didn't matter. He would shape me into a thinking-functioning quarterback. Our first scrimmage was a rain game. We played at Tuloso-Midway. It was hard to hold onto the football, it sort of was like a "rite of passage." I got better and better. When we played against Beeville at their stadium, I finally felt like a winner. We called one of our pass plays. It was a "bomb" to one of my friends. It hits him in the hands and he drops it! As he's coming back to the sideline, Coach Cruz calls him over. He says, Neal! BUTTERFINGERS!!! I didn't hear this, but Neal told me later on. He also told me that Cruz told him that it was going to be right there in his hands. That game there would be three that did hit his hands and he scored each time. I managed to throw two more TD passes other receivers. One was a "fingertip" catch that I would remind that kid later all through high school. I'd say, "Hey, you remember?" I could see it in his eyes reliving the moment.

Coach Cruz was quite a character. One time at practice, our center Noel, was practicing his deep snaps to the punter. Unknowingly, Cruz walks between the center and punter and gets drilled in the side of the head with the football. It knocks off his glasses and he looks pissed. He turns and looks at Noel and says, "Noel, get out FOREVER! He runs off to the sidelines then Coach immediately calls him back. We're all cracking up laughing.

Another time he tells a lineman who missed his block, he said, Rosas they give you a first down, what more do you want, HAMBURGERS?

Coach Cruz was gutsy. We were playing San Diego at our practice field there at William Adams. He calls "the bomb" on the first play, and yes we scored! The play was actually called, B-Right, Sprint out Tough. I was gaining more and more confidence. It was fun to win and win we did. We played a Junior Varsity team from George West, a small town north of Alice. We were freshmen and they were juniors! What were they thinking! It was the hardest hitting game ever. We did lose, but we gave them a good run. We were on our own one-yard line when the Coach calls 544, a dive play. Our halfback, Joe, was a little guy, but super-fast. He took the ball and broke through and ran for a 99 yard touchdown! We were ecstatic!

Once in high school, most of us were on the junior varsity team. There were a couple of players who made the varsity, but I could not compete at that level just yet. It was tough. All of the teams were bigger than us in size. We were all mostly sophomores and had to play smart and our offense had quite a bit of miss direction. Our jerseys were burnt orange so it camouflaged the ball somewhat. Late in the season we played the Ben Bolt varsity team. To date, that was the hardest hitting game so far. They played dirty. That is to say that they scratched, pinched and punched. We were behind 8-0 with a few seconds left on the clock. We call a pass play to move the ball up the field closer to the goal line. He, Neal catches the pass and he gets roughed up and they call a penalty. Now there is zero seconds left on the clock, but we get one more play. In the huddle I told the line just to give me three seconds. I call the pass play to Neal. As I roll out I throw the ball as far as I can. We were on their 30 yard line. He catches the ball, but is off balance and about to fall forward, short of the goal line. A player comes and hits him from behind and that straightens him up and he then is able to run across the goal line! We had to go for the two points. I give the ball to a junior who was playing his first year of football. He was a big guy and there was nothing that was going to stop him from getting into the end zone. We tied!

I got moved to the varsity the following year. I would also learn the linebacker position, but I was an offense person. I would be the back-up QB for three games, but was not happy. I asked the Coach to move me down to the JV so that I could play. They did and it was much better. I was thinking more. I had a thing with the center, who by the way had been so since my freshman year, that if there was an opening, I would pinch him on the side that I wanted him to go leading the way. Well, it just so happened that in Kingsville, there was a play called, and the two linebackers were going to stunt the center guard gap, but then went over to the guard tackle gap which left no one right in front of me. I pinched the center and off we went down the field 35 yards for a QB sneak TD!

At the beginning of my senior year I was still only sixteen years old and wouldn't turn seventeen until December. I was the youngest student in my class and when I was a sophomore, I was the youngest kid in school. I, however, have always competed with my older peers in my class and those a year ahead of me. I learned at an early age that I could do as well as anyone as long as I worked hard, which I did. I knew that I would be in a good position to start at QB my senior year and was prepared to do so.

Prior to the season starting, all of the sport writers in the area, mostly Corpus predicted our team, Alice, to be last in our district. No matter. We still trained hard.

On our first scrimmage game against Gregory-Portland I got hammered on every play. They were a big bunch of guys and way outsized us. Near the end of the game I got a concussion. It was written in the paper that I had gotten my "bell rung." I would say it was more than that. After that loss and the next two I started to think that I couldn't help but think that maybe they were right.

On our third game against Falfurrias it all came together. I would be running the 300 series which was the "triple option." I would have to "read" the defensive tackle. He would tell me whether to leave the ball with the fullback or pull it. This read is a split-second fast all the while trying to avoid getting killed. I would then attack the defensive end. We had a star running back and as soon as he was passed the end, I would "pitch" the ball to him and it was off to the races! If the end went for my pitch man, then I would tuck the ball and be off to the races myself. I got good at "reading." We won our first game which gave us much needed confidence. The first two losses didn't matter since they weren't district games.

Our first district game was a tough loss, but we did get better as a team and I scored the only TD thanks to our awesome offensive line. That would be our only district loss. We kept surprising our opponents, especially those who underestimated us. There were several times when I would call an audible there at the line of scrimmage if I saw something and had to adjust. I checked off plays three times for touchdowns.

About halfway through the season I got hurt. I had pulled the ball and was running down field when my ankle got caught between two players. It was in the fourth quarter and we had to use the back-up QB who wasn't really a QB, he wanted to be a QB so badly too. He did make a better safety. They ended up pulling up the QB from the JV who was indeed a QB, and a good one at that.

I practiced lightly the following week. My ankle was still very tender. On the day of the game I went to the Dr.'s office and they shot up my ankle with cortisone, like in the movie, *North Dallas Forty,* but on my ankle. Shit, that did the trick! No more pain. At the game, I was carrying out a fake and the defensive player "bull-dogged" me to the ground and my ankle got twisted again and had to leave the game. As I'm coming off of the field I told the Coach that 419 would be wide open. He called it and my replacement QB scored a TD on his very first varsity play. We would split time at QB after that. I ran the ground game with throwing maybe one or two passes a game, but we would rush for over five hundred yards in many games. We did make the Texas state playoffs. We were District Co-Champions with Corpus Christi Carroll, but we had defeated them so we got to represent the district. That was back when only one team represented. Now, there are maybe three or four that get to go to the playoffs.

In the playoffs we beat Edinburgh by a few points barely for the Bi-District game. Next, was the Regional game against "Austin Reagan." By this time there would be only sixteen teams still going in all of Texas. Pretty bfd! We would play in a neutral the site of Victoria, Texas, coincidentally, where I now live. The grass was way too high. I would have rather played in our field or Texas Memorial Stadium. I would have chosen the latter. Reagan had some big boys and had us on size. We would lose 31-13 and that would make our fourth loss for the season. We finished with an 8-4 record.

In Alice the senior Varsity players get to play the upcoming Varsity team for the next season. It would be the last time that I would get to play. The new guys kept telling us how bad they were going to beat us. Nope. We would win and I would finish my football career with a win!

I did get Honorable Mention at quarterback and several players made All-South Texas and or All-American. My friend Donny, who was our eighth grade QB, made All-American as a guard. We did get to prove all of the sport writers of the Corpus Christi Caller WRONG! **Sidebar:** Being a vivid and lucid dreamer, I dreamed that I had quit football at the beginning of my senior year. I was finished with the BS. In one dream my friends and I are in a parade in the back of a truck wearing our jerseys. I said, what the hell are we doing? We were going to be playing the varsity team and us as old guys against them. I thought we're going to get massacred, I hope we don't die! Sometimes I have to remember that I DID play.

As an eighth grader I also played basketball one year. I would make the B-Team. We didn't even have orange or white uniforms. They were green and used to belong to Memorial Junior High, there in town when it used to be a junior high. The uniforms were quite old. I would never play organized basketball again.

    I also ran track and the only reason I had gone out for basketball and track was because all of my friends did. I ran the 880, which was two laps. It was a very tough race to run. At our district meet called the *Hub City Relays,* my friends and I had gone to eat lunch at the town's new burger joint, called Burger Chef. I knew that my race started at two o'clock and it was only twelve so, I had time to let my food digest. I had eaten a big burger and was so stuffed. I felt awful. When I got back to the stadium, everyone had been looking for me. They had "bumped up" my tine to one o'clock. Oh snap! I am quickly given my number and the gun goes off! Bang! I'm off and still can't believe that I'm running. I'm on the inside lane and when we even up after the turn I just turn it up and take the lead right away. I hold my lead throughout the race and when I crossed the finish line the second place runner was just coming around the last turn! I had a school record of 2.11.2 seconds. It was an eighth grade record in Alice for a few years, but has since been broken. I never did run track after that.

3. Higher Education

I just want to say that I was a very lucky kid who had parents who gave a damn and taught me to be an independent person. I know that they did the best that they knew how at that time in their lives. I really didn't know what I wanted to do I just knew that I would be doing it in college somewhere.

I got a call from one of my friends who attended the University of Texas. She was a former cheerleader there in Alice and called me trying to recruit me into attending UT. I had no desire to be in a place that humongous. I wanted to go to a smaller college.

I had graduated from high school, as I mentioned, with still no plan of action. I did play in a Big-League baseball All-Star game that summer in San Antonio. The Hill Junior College baseball coach was there. I introduced myself and he invited me to play at Hill. One of my friends had attended there the previous year. That was it! I would play baseball and see where it would take me.

I kissed my mother goodbye as I left in my Datsun F10 to pick up my roommate, Raúl. I had never even been to the campus. It was about a five-hour drive from Alice. My car was packed to the max. I did have my stereo and speakers in there. We pull into the campus. The dorms that we are going to stay in are brand new and they are co-ed!

So, there I am registering and the lady asks me, "What's your major?" I had no freaking clue! Knowing about sports, but not wanting to be a coach, I said P.E.! I start taking all these P.E. classes and the basics of course. I had enrolled in eighteen hours. It seemed normal then, but as a grad student, it would be unheard of. It's an exciting time, new faces, girls and adventures.

I got ready for my first day of class. I would be going to my history class first. I was in college now, right? You can wear whatever you want. So, I put on my green Birdwell Beach Britches on and wore them to class. Upon entering with a smile, the teacher, Mr. Smith, yelled at me saying, "I'm not here to teach beach class! Get out of here and go change!" What the ....? I couldn't believe what had just happened! I walked out of the class feeling puny and went back to my dorm. I thought, Fuck him, that asshole! I'm not going back! Then I thought, no. If I don't return, I'll come out looking like a chicken-shit. So, I changed into some jeans and returned back to class. I slowly opened the door, peeked in, walked in, then I slammed it shut with all of my might! It shook the whole room and was very, very loud. I quietly walked over and took my seat. I sat there and got up to leave when the bell rang. The teacher walked over to me and politely apologized. His hands were shaking. I think he thought that I might want to kick his wimpy ass. He did buy me a couple of beers at the State Fair in Dallas a month later!

My grandmother wanted me to attend Texas A & I in Kingsville, but that was way too close to home, about twenty miles away. Anyway, I already went there when I was a sophomore and junior in high school. My friends and I would skip school and go hang out there during the day, but make it back for afternoon football practice. I enjoyed being away from home. Life was an adventure!

At Hill, I played baseball during the fall season. There were players from everywhere, New York, Florida, El Paso, San Antonio and Alice! All I wanted was a chance to play. At this point the coach had his returning starters who he favored. It only makes sense since he already knows what they can do. Unknowns like me had to really make a big impression. I did have some hits. One of those was from a ninety-five MPH fastball from a big black pitcher from Paul Quinn University. The competition was stiff. We would run the "loop" and "superloop" during the off-season for conditioning. I didn't get too much playing time, and did not make the team for the regular season. I was a bit disappointed. I would be going somewhere different next year.

A CHICANO SPANISH TEACHER

Hillsboro was in Hill County, a dry county where they did not sell any alcohol. We had to drive fifteen miles south on Interstate 35 to West. I had always been the driver since I was twelve years old because it's always been my car. Well, on one Wednesday night they had 25 cent pitchers of beer, I just got totally shit-faced. I don't like to get drunk. I don't like the feeling. But, anyway we were getting ready to return to our dorm and I started to get in the driver's seat and my friend from El Paso, Polo, said, "No, let me drive." I said, no at first, but then relented and let him drive. On the way, I told him to pull over off to the side of the road because I needed to hurl. They had just finished that portion of I35 and just off the shoulder was a steep drop down. It was wet because it had been raining and on the slope off of the shoulder, there was only dirt, now mud. I slipped all the way down to the bottom of the side of the road. I tried to climb up and I would slide back down and I was drunk on top of that. After much struggling I made it to the top and back to my car. I got in and shut the door. We got back to the dorm and later in the morning I went to check my car and it had these huge chunks of mud on the passenger side floorboard. I just put my muddy clothes in my duffle bag and didn't wash them until I went home a couple of weeks later. My mom was pissed.

My friends and I went to a strip club in Waco called Rocky Racoon's. I was only seventeen, but they still let me in. It was my first time ever. What fun! Naked girls dancing! I got in line to give the stripper some money and slipped a dollar in her g-string and turned to walk away when she grabbed my head and pulled me toward her and gave me a five second frencher! Wow! What fun!

One night when we came back to campus after drinking my friends and I decided that it would be a great idea if we climbed the water tower on campus. We turned off my car lights and sneaked in over the fence. We were all drunk. What morons! We all climbed up to the top walked around and smoked a couple of doobies and climbed down without getting caught or killed. How lucky we were!

In the Spring I would have new roommates Patrick and Gil. Patrick was an Irish guy, originally from Brooklyn, NY, now living in Arlington, TX. He liked music as well. When some friends and I went to a concert at Tarrant County Convention Center in Fort Worth to see Cheap Trick and Foreigner, my car was full except for the hatchback part. He said he would ride there if I would let him. I did. We also went to see Queen, Nazareth, Thin Lizzy, Boston and Sammy Hagar in Dallas and Fort Worth.

One weekend I went with him to Arlington. He drove a little red Toyota four-wheel drive truck. We drove by a motocross race track. He drives in and starts to drive the course, hauling ass over all the bumps and moguls. We come around the corner and some guys come out and signals for us to stop. Duffy stops and he tells us we have to leave and Patrick peels out and the guy throws the bottle he has in his hand at the back of his windshield. Thank God it doesn't shatter and we finally get out. On the way back to Hillsboro, Duffy is hauling and a DPS officer flashes him to stop. The DPS is on the other side of the highway. Patrick exits and drives into town and pulls into a driveway in a neighborhood with his lights out. We see the DPS go by and wait a bit before returning to the dorm. This was the summer of '79 and I just had gone through one year of college. I wanted to attend the Texxas World Music Festival or if you like, The Texxas Jam once again. This time, my friend Gary would make the drive up to Dallas with me. We went to the concert and drove back to Hillsboro, where we spent the night at my girlfriend's house, which would be the last time that I would see her. We left for Alice and somewhere between Hillsboro and Alice, I'm not sure where, but I fell asleep at the wheel! I'm lucky that there was a big space between the road and the fence line. I came to about fifteen yards from the fence and managed to steer the car back onto the highway. Gary had fallen asleep too. It scared the crap out of me! Thank you God!

I transferred to Texas Southmost College and the same thing happened, with regards to baseball sort of. Coach Silva of CC Moody had just been hired to coach baseball at Texas Southmost College in Brownsville. I got an invitation to his home along with a bunch of other players for a party. I would give it a go to play baseball once more. Also attending TSC were other players from Alice. They had all just graduated. It would be five of us sharing a big studio apartment in Brownsville. This was the fall of 1979. Once again, I played the fall season, but did not make the team. I was not used to this. I just didn't make a big impression. I decided that I would concentrate on my education for once!

While in Brownsville in '79, it was the height of the disco era and there was way more stuff to do there in Brownsville. One of the main streets in town, Central Ave, I think, had quite a few bars and discos. We would all go, even though I've always been a rocker, it was where all the girls would go, and rockers like the girls.

There at Southmost I had taken courses like weight-lifting. I would have gotten an A in the class, but I had to do thirty pull-ups and could only do twenty-nine! I also took paddle tennis and table tennis or ping pong. I was my class champ for table tennis. We had a round-robin tournament and I was the last person standing. So, with no one on the other side to serve the ball to, I hit the ball down hard to make it bounce high across to the other side. That gives me time to run around and slam the ball when it bounces up. It's in, I win!

I was still a P.E. major, but I had taken a Psychology class with Dr. James and then with Dr. Freeman. It was so damn interesting to me. She was pretty easy on the eyes too. I had taken a British Lit class with a male teacher, can't remember his name, but I got an F. I re-took the class with a woman professor. She was a tall woman, with short red hair and was so passionate about her subject. It fired me up. She told us all a story about when she was getting out of a cab in New York City and that some guy tried to grab her purse. It scared her and all she could do was hold on to the purse and drag the guy with her until he let go. I got an A in her class. I learned so much and still love Wordsworth, Coleridge and Donne.

I already had quite a few P.E. courses like Kinesiology. It helped that I took Physiology in high school. I knew that I didn't want to be a coach, until I did later on. I would be in Brownsville for two years. I enjoyed it. Weed was really cheap! We would go across the border to eat lunch almost daily. It was a cool onda. There were no problems at all with gangs like there might be now.

On one of my drives home for the weekend, I was going up on Highway 77 up around Sarita. There was a school bus pulled over on the opposite of the road. There were two men flagging me down. I was in no hurry, so I pulled over and parked behind the bus. It was an older man and a young Asian guy. They were polite and thanked me for pulling over. They asked me if I could spare any gas. My car was right above empty, so I told them that I couldn't, sorry. Then the older guy asked me if I had some, and he puts his two fingers together like he's smoking a joint. That I had! I passed them some, but I didn't have any papers. They said no problem. They were so happy and I felt good about stopping. You never know when it's going to be you needing some assistance, a nice little deposit to my Karma account.

On another weekend drive home up from the Rio Grande Valley to Alice, my mother and brother were driving along with me. I can't recall the reason why. **Confession:** I got my mother stoned! I think this was in 1980. On the drive up I told my mother instead of listening to people talk negatively about weed that have never tried it, why not try it yourself? She had always ragged on me about my smoking weed, and still does. I'm a grown ass man! I'm not a bad person! It's not a moral thing like so many have equated it in the past. I'd rather be friends with a nice pot smoker than a crook in a suit. Back to the story, I had rolled three sinsemilla joints. This was pretty potent stuff, way more than the first stuff I had tried years before. I told her to smoke a whole one and gave it to her. My brother was in the backseat just watching in amazement as to what was going on. We got home later that afternoon and she went to bed and fell asleep fast, and slept the whole following day! I can't believe I got my mom stoned! My new focus was to concentrate on picking up my grades.

A CHICANO SPANISH TEACHER

I had a good Psychology professor for the second half of General Psychology. Dr. Freeman was her name. I was really attracted to her and so was my roommate Vince. He also played baseball and we've known each other since we were eleven years old in Little League. She really got me interested in Psychology, so much that I kept taking Psychology classes. I had a Sex Education teacher who was excellent also. His name was Bill and he made sure to tell the class that he was Jewish. I didn't care one way or the other. For our first class he put us in groups of four or five and gave each group a paper sack. He told us to get the clay out and shape a penis and a vagina with it as a group. Dang! That was breaking the ice! He was so cool. I learned so much from him. My English girlfriend was taking the class with me and she was very smart and we studied together. She was gorgeous and taller than me with blue eyes. Oh, she taught me a lot too. Luckily for me, she was multi-orgasmic and quite enthusiastic! She followed me to San Marcos, I thought she would be going to Austin attending UT. She already wanted to get married and have kids, while I still thought that I was a kid and not yet ready. We went our separate ways and remained friends. She did marry a millionaire from Mexico City! I really was happy for her.

I ended up getting a Certificate of Completion and not an Associate Degree due to lacking one class, College Algebra. I would take it at Southwest.

I moved to San Marcos in 1981 with sixty credit hours. On my drive up to Hillsboro a couple of years back, we would drive through San Marcos, hitting Interstate 35. It looked so green and natural and a cool place to go to school. At last, I was moving up to San Marcos and decided that it would be more cost effective if I stayed in a travel trailer. My father got me a 17-foot Used Prowler. It would do. It had cold a/c and the price was right. I lived there at United Campgrounds in San Marcos for two years. The monthly rent for a slot was $72 plus electricity and water was free. The trailer had everything I needed. It would be much cheaper than living with roommates in an apartment. I had just gotten out of that situation, although it wasn't too bad. I prefer to live alone and go and come as I please. The campground was clean and well-managed. They had a laundromat, a swimming pool and showers. They even had a ping-pong table! I played with different people that I had met there at the campgrounds. I had a problem one time with the water pump in my trailer and I asked the owner/manager if he could see what the problem was. He fixed it and didn't even charge me. He was kind and fair. It didn't take him long to figure it out.

I met quite a few people living there at United Campgrounds. One of the characters was Joe. Actually, his name was Joel. He was a young-looking guy who was a Vietnam Vet. He was divorced and had children. He missed his kids a lot and would show me pictures. He lived in a tent in the next row of spaces. We would go to the river and cook stuff together. He was a good guy dealt a tough hand. On through the years every so often, I would see him at the river. My brother would also see him at the river years later.

Another couple that I met was this Italian-Greek couple from up north, Chicago I think. His name was Bob, but everyone called him Herky, short for Hercules. He had a family of five and lived in a trailer smaller than mine! He was a body man. He was always hustling to get some work. My friend had just met him there at the campgrounds when he was visiting me. Brent had a dent in his car door and Herky told him that he could fix it in no time. Brent said Ok. Herky went to the trunk of his car and took out his tool. He started putting a hole in the door to be able to yank it back out into place. Brent's eyes opened up wide as he didn't expect that. He's probably thinking, "What the fuck?" He fixed it soon enough and smooth out with some bondo.

Another time, I was with Herky and we were driving on Post Road heading for five-mile dam. It was five miles away, oh wow! After turning left under the railroad trestle there was a one-lane bridge. When we got there to the bridge we couldn't pass because there was a car blocking the road. Now Herky is darker than me and shorter with a long black beard. He has a Chicago accent and he looks a little intimidating, except for his size. Around the car, there are all these frat guys. I know what a frat guy looks like. There were about ten of them standing around the car. I think they had a head on collision and the other had apparently taken off. Herky and I walk over and they ALL get puffy-chested. Herky says, "Hey what's going on here? No one seems to fucking know anything. The hood is dented and they can't get it open. Herky walks over and bangs on the hood real hard and pops it open. They are all fucking stunned! He tells the guy to get into the car and try to start it. Herky does something to the engine and the car starts. All of the guys' jaws drop. Herky then tells them to "move this piece of shit of a car out of here so that we can move on through!"

Back at the trailer, the a/c worked very well, the bed was comfortable and I had hot water, a stove and a small fridge. Eventually I got a phone, a landline. That was the only kind back then in 1981! I also had my portable black and white television that my grandmother gave me one Christmas. For only having an antenna, I had great reception in San Marcos. I could get the Austin and San Antonio stations including PBS.

I brought my English racer bike that I've had since I was twelve years old. I would ride it from United Campgrounds which was east of Interstate 35 and turn on to Aquarena Springs Drive. Once I hit Aquarena I could coast since it was a little downhill all the way to campus. Once I got to campus, the first time I rode my bike up the hill by the Education building. Fuck! It was so freaking hard! People were walking up the hill faster than I was going on the bike, and when I finally made it to the top, it felt like my thighs were the size of Robert Newhouse's, a former running back from the Dallas Cowboys and Houston Cougars. After that first time, I decided to park my bike at the J.C. Kellam building. It used to be the library. It's at the bottom of the hill.

Across Interstate 35 from United Campground where I lived was the club Animal House. I would just walk across the highway jumping over the rail in the median, it wasn't that high. Of course, I had to watch out for traffic. On some nights you could get all you could drink for $5! People would get so shit-faced. I have never liked to get drunk or never intended it to happen. At closing I wouldn't have to drive since I lived across the highway, yea!

Another place that my friends and I would frequent was Showdowns in San Marcos. It was a small bar near the campus off of LBJ. We would go there for lunch and have half a ham and cheese sandwich, with a dill spear, a few chips and a beer, all for only $1.50! Good deal! I went there with my friends to celebrate my twenty-first birthday. They ordered me some flaming armadillos and kamikazes. I got so drunk and when I was at home throwing up, I could feel a piece of spongy-fatty tissue I dislodged in my throat. I had to have it surgically removed.

My mother was living in San Antonio and working for an ENT. They sent me to Memorial Medical Center there in SA. **Confession:** I had taken one doobie with me to the hospital. I would be there for five days. I would open the window and sit on the ledge outside of it. I would take a couple of hits, then put it out. I did this a few times until I finished it. Late night I would get the munchies and order something to eat and they would bring it. No one ever said anything!

When it came time for Wurstfest, my brother would come up and I think even my mom went with us once. I used to go with my friends on College Night you wouldn't believe all of the girls. They would just walk around and ask if you wanted a "Wurstfest Kiss?" Hell yeah! They were usually pretty girls at that. I got brave and even asked a couple of girls for one, to which they obliged me. We would walk around with a stack of beer cups with the Wurstfest logo. The food was always so good. One time I went into the big hall where there was a long wooden bar. As I ordered my drink, I look to the right and see none other than Flaco Jimenez! I said, wow! Living legend! Mr. Flaco Jimenez! He shook my hand and I told him that I was a fan. He had had a couple already and was feeling mighty good. It was so cool to see him there. Talk about unexpected.

One of my friends, Brent, was also from Alice. I recognized him as he was in the same Physics class as me. We met and became pretty good friends. I would go and visit him at his apartment which was just down Aquarena Springs Drive. He always had good smoke and quite a variety of it as well. He had asked me if I wanted a job. **Confession:** Though, it's not really a confession since it's a legit job, but thought I would include it anyway. He was working at a place called Western News, it was an adult bookstore. Lou, our boss, lived at the same apartment complex as Grant and they needed someone. I needed a job as well, so I took it. I would work there for two years as I was finishing up my Bachelor's degree. It gave me ample time to study while I was working as a clerk, but not for the first couple of weeks! After that I was so desensitized that I never looked at another girlie magazine as long as I worked there. It was interesting, the people that would come in to the store. One time a couple came and bought some lingerie. The woman had gone to the restroom in the back and came back out to the front to ask me what I thought. I just said, nice. Quite a few gay guys would come in. They were cool. One guy did call on the phone during my shift and asked if he could blow me. I said no thanks. I like girls. I had a beautiful girlfriend at that. I quit working just before I graduated since I'd be teaching Spanish at the University.

I was taking a senior level Psychology class called Group Process with Dr. Jarrad. It was an interesting class. However, we could only speak in the here-and-now. We couldn't talk about our history or past or anything that didn't include the entire group. What? Yes, it was difficult. What started us talking about the group came about when there was this one female student, Wendy, who came in late three days in a row. This prompted one girl in class to tell her that she was rude to the class by being late and then this other guy starts telling her that he didn't believe that she should be wearing all that makeup! He said that his family, were Quakers and that they didn't believe in wearing makeup. Now this girl is pretty and looks like a sorority girl, because she is! Yes, she came late and yes, she did wear makeup, but who in the fuck did they think they were? She was otherwise nice and pleasant. I had to say something. I said, you don't know if she had to take a friend to the hospital because no one else was able to, or you don't know if she went by the groceries to pick up some food for an elderly neighbor and yet she still came to class. How many of you would have just blown off class? And you, I was speaking to the guy, who cares about your family and what they think, they aren't here are they? What if I said, that my family didn't believe in people wearing glasses as he, was wearing. It sounds pretty dumb now doesn't it? Well, the tardy girl didn't come in tardy anymore after that. I did see Wendy at Wurstfest later that year. She was with her group of friends, girls and guys both. I said hi to her and asked her, hey how about a Wurstfest kiss? She said, no. Then I leaned over and whispered, none of these jokers defended you like I did. She then, grabs my head and gives me a big freaking kiss in front of everyone! As I was walking away, I heard one of them ask her, who was that?

When my girlfriend moved in, we lived in the trailer for a couple of months. One day my friend Joe told me he wanted to show me something. So we got in my car and drove through San Marcos on Hopkins St. We turned right on Bishop and then made a left on the very next street. We drove to the end of the street to a dirt road leading up to the right. I went up a little and parked. We walked a short way and saw a fenced in area. It had a high fence with barbed-wire on top. We climbed over the fence and saw a cave opening. At the opening there was a big boulder with a sign that said "Ezell's Cave." Just a little further in was another smaller bolder with a water hose tied around it and leading down about fifteen feet or so. We all climbed down into a big room. It was dark and we all had flashlights. Mine was a waterproof one. We saw a very narrow trail and decided to have a look. We were going down in elevation and everything was sort of damp. We had to crawl through in couple of spots and made it to another room. I shined my light out front and you could see this crystal-clear water. It was the freaking Edwards Aquifer~! I then turned off my flashlight and then so did the other two and it was so dark we could not see our hands in front of our faces. We then took a little swim, but we didn't want to contaminate the water so we didn't stay in too long. It was so clear! It was a little slippery trying to climb back out. Now that we were wet, we were going to get a little muddy going back. We made it back to the opening where the water hose was. Joe climbed up easily. I let my girlfriend go next, but she couldn't pull herself up. I went up easily then Joe and I would pull her up. I told her to hold on tight and we pulled her up. Pulling up dead weight is not very easy. We got her up and now had a little story to tell.

San Marcos was a great place to go to college. The San Marcos River runs through the campus. It's beautiful. Many students hang out and sunbathe there at Sewell Park. Often there are car accidents because people (guys) are rubber necking checking out all the hot co-eds on the hill.

Early on when I moved to San Marcos I had my brother, Adrian, come down and stay for a while. He would bring Benji, our dog along with him. We would go to the river. At first, he asked, Can we bring the dog? I said, are you kidding, of course! He's going to be such a babe magnet you won't believe your eyes. Sure enough, we all went to the river and hung around the falls area first. There was a good drop off from the wall down to the river. Perhaps about an eight foot drop. After we all dove in the chilly water, Benji couldn't stand not being with us, so he jumped too. All the girls around gave him quite a bit of attention. It was so much fun. We would also go down to White Water Sports, near Canyon Lake and camp out and float the Guadalupe River. The first time my brother came up to go camping we didn't have anything to camp with. We went to Kimbo's for some of their fried chicken and wedge fries. Oh, they tasted so good. We went back and slept on the windshield of my car. My mother met us there and brought some food and camping gear. We would tube the Guadalupe River also. It's quite cold, but you get used to it eventually. We always took an ice chest and some smoke to enjoy the scenery. It's really beautiful. One time going over a dam, Benji fell out of the tube and I had to reach back as far as I could to grab him. Those were some good times!

The San Marcos River is the perfect tubing trip. It only takes about an hour or so depending on the current. The water is clear and is a cool 72 degrees year-round! In the winter time when it's very cold, freezing or below, you can see the steam coming up from the river. We used to go on tubing trips at night. It was kind of spooky, but when girls want to go, what you gonna do? For my Scuba Advanced Open Water certification, we had to dive the San Marcos River at night. The river begins at Spring Lake and there are "falls" that churn the water and make a strong current. We stayed along the wall and went underneath the building. There was a restaurant on top called Peppers at the Falls. Underneath we could see quite a few fresh water eels. They look way different than morays. We also saw some spotted gar and plenty of fish and turtles. The snorkeling there in the river was great too.

One of my professors, Dr. Jones would go to the river and swim against the current. He was an older guy, witty and in great condition. That river always has a good current. I've seen it raging when it flooded and got as high as just under the signal lights at the intersection there at the bridge.

We moved out to the country where we would live in a cottage. The price was right all I had to do was work fourteen hours a week for my rent. It was just north of San Marcos off of Lime Kiln Rd. I had more sweat than dinero at the time and besides, I've always wanted to live out in the country.

My first week there Mr. Harris taught me how everything worked, how and where to feed the seven dogs, thirteen cats, and several cows and bulls. I learned about the windmill, the overflow and shut-off lever, where all the different types of tools were, etc. After a week, the Harris' took off on vacation in their travel trailer for a couple of months. They must have had a lot of confidence in me. I love dogs and cats anyway so that was easy. There was no else around but my girlfriend and I. We did take a blanket out to the woods and found a nice spot under a tree. It was so nice.

There at the ranch there was always something that had to be done. First, I would go to the barn and feed the cows and bulls. They all had their own buckets! At first I would have to grind some milo grain and dried corn by hand, then put it in their buckets. This was a lot of labor, but better than paying $$$ for my rent! Later on, Mr. Harris started giving the cows feed cubes instead and not so labor intensive. He had a big black Brangus bull. It didn't have horns, just little nubs. He was humongous. He looked more like a buffalo, and he was the sweetest bull that I've ever known, very gentle. There was also a red bull. It had horns that stuck straight out and he was a mean son of a bitch. When it came time to feed them, he was always quite aggressive in getting his bucket. He would then try and eat the other cow's bucket. I always had to keep them separated in the barn. There were several stalls where I could easily do this. It was scary though. He ended up selling the big bull. He was jumping over the neighbors' fences to get the cows. He was a lover, not a fighter. He was also tearing down the fences, which we had to repair. I was sad to see him go. Mr. Harris told me that one of the cows didn't show up to eat in the morning. He asked me to go and look for it. There was 130 acres out there. Where do you start? I took a look out towards the land from the driveway atop a hill where his house is. I saw some buzzards flying over in one direction and decided to head out that way. On the way I saw a family of little baby armadillos. They were so cute! I eventually found the baby calf, still wet from just being born. I was about three hundred yards from the barn. So, I decided to carry the baby calf back to the barn. The mother cow was nearby and followed closely. I had to stop a couple of times to rest as it got a little heavy. I did make it back to the barn and was able to keep them separated from the other cows. We had to bottle feed the calf. For some reason it wouldn't feed on its own. The cow's teats looked like they were getting ready to burst, with a little milk leaking out. Mr. Harris asked if I could milk them and demonstrated how. These weren't milk cows. They weren't used to humans touching them in that way. It must have been awkward for the cow because I just put a bucket down and sat by the cow. I talked to her, telling her that she was brave to let me get milk for her baby. As I squeezed in a downward pull of the "lever" I could feel the milk pouring back in where it would fill and I could continue to squeeze it out. I filled a bucket pretty quickly. We named him Ivan. He would let me brush him while he ate. Then he became a bull and we started calling him Ivan the Terrible. He got aggressive and Mr. Harris had me take him to the auction in Lockhart. I had already gone before with Mr. Harris, so I knew the drill. Sadly when I opened up the trailer for him to get out, he did, and turned to look at me, and had a tear running down his cheek. I felt bad for him. But I could count that as time for my rent, easy time. Otherwise, it was hard work.

Something else I had to do was paint two houses. That means you have to scrape, prime, then paint. I got to use a sprayer on a compressor which made it easier and faster. I also sandblasted the water tank where the well-water was stored. I mowed like there was no tomorrow, and cut trees like I was Paul Bunyan, just a bit shorter. There were oak trees all around that were dead due to oak decline. I cut the dead ones in his yard first. They were huge! I used a twenty-four inch chainsaw. I became quite good at it. I would then cut the tree down and chop it up for firewood. I watered and spread cow manure in the garden every spring. I also got to share in the harvest. He had many peach trees, some fig trees, a pear tree and a plum tree. They all produced and he even had some grapes growing as well. There were blackberries, okra, tomatoes, corn and squash.

I changed majors from Physical Education to Psychology. I had all these psych classes and I thought I might as well change my major. I did also take some intermediate Spanish classes like 2310 and 2320. One of my favorite professors was Dr. Galvez. He had already retired and was teaching part-time. He was so smart and such a decent person. He wrote poetry for his wife, how romantic! He got his Ph. D when he was twenty-three years old from Tulane University! Wow! He was so cool. He wrote dictionaries.

I was the typical Chicano who thought they knew Spanish. When we got our papers back, I looked at my C. Then I glance over at the little gringuitas making A's. Whaaat? It's called studying! I did get better and studied more, especially in the advanced classes. Some of my other favorite professors were Dr. Paez, Dr. Torres, Dr. Jones and Dr. Carlton. I was in Dr. Torres's class when her water broke. Oh snap! I ran downstairs to the Dept. of Modern Language office and told Mrs. Salas, the secretary about the situation.

Dr. Paez was a great cook. She made our class a couple of "tortillas españolas." They were delicious! It's like an omelet pie, good stuff. My favorite classes were the Spanish Civilization and Latin American Civilization classes that I had with Drs. Pablos and Jones.

I also took Psychology classes that were recommended if you were going to graduate school. So, I took History and Theory, Learning and Memory, Brain and Behavior, and other classes. The Psychology Dept. had a brand new building with three levels. As I was waiting in the hallway between classes like everyone else, this one girl has one of those long sheer earth momma skirts and proceeds to sit "Indian Style" with her legs crossed. She does that and has no underwear on! I turn and look and my friend sitting next to me to check if he saw. He did. Dang, the things you see on a college campus, just another one of God's little gifts.

I was excited to take an Abnormal Psychology class. The professor was Dr. Shylo. She was a brilliant teacher. I learned so much from her. We had the option of having two-thirds of our grade include non-test material. We could get a grade for doing the assigned study guides and extra-credit if you did all of them. You could also do volunteer work at different places. I decided to go that route. I did all of the study guides and the extra ones too. When it was time to check them and my grade with her in her office, she told me that I got credit for the ones that I turned in, but not the extra ones. She said that I did not do them. I told her that I did. I knew for sure that I did! She told me that she didn't make mistakes like that. I told her that I would be back. I rushed back home and retrieved my extra study guide chapters. I went into her office and threw them on her desk. You see I told you, I said. She was like "well I, I, I," I said, just give me my grade.

On the first day of class with Dr. Shylo, I'm sitting on the second or third row of long tables and in walked this blonde beauty. She asked me if she could sit next to me! I was like, uh, yeah. Her name was Kayleigh and she was stunning. She came out in the Miss

Texas Beauty Pageant that year. On one class day, I was looking up front at the professor and I felt something come up from underneath the table and it was Kayleigh's hand reaching for my watch to see what time it was! It was chilling, she was so classy. On my first test in there I thought that I had studied and knew the material, but when I received my 54, I was shocked. I couldn't believe it. I had studied hard, or so I thought. I did begin making A's and Kayleigh had asked me if I would study with her. I told her sure. I had a few study groups that I was in. It helped my learning.

I did decide that I would go and check out the Crisis Hotline Center, one of the places we could volunteer at. It was in the Campus Christian Community building. The person running the hotline was an LPC Counselor named Cheryl, one very cool lady and an excellent ping-pong player.

For our training we met in a building and in the room where we were there were blank posters on all of the walls. We had to go up and write all of the slang words for coitus, penis, vagina and I can't remember what else. After everyone finished, it was kind of fun, they had us go around and say what we had written. The very first guy they called on stood up and calmly said, "F U C K Y O U!" Everyone laughed. The job was mostly giving out information and referrals. But, one day I got a suicide call and Cheryl immediately got up and walked out of the room! What the fu....? I told her that I had a suicide call and she walked away. So, I spoke with this fifty-four year old woman who was alone at home and felt ignored. I kept reassuring her that she was an important and valuable person. I told her how she could affect another person just with her smile. It could be someone who is in a bad place and would appreciate it more than she could ever know. I spoke with that lady for two whole hours! It was exhausting. You don't know. Oh Lordy! I worked there for the semester, but would go and visit every so often. They had good lunches on Wednesdays. I would go on Peace and Nuclear Freeze marches with them in Austin. At one of the protests, we were walking behind the Palestinian Liberation

Organization (PLO) and in front of the Black Panthers. What an experience! I did make an A in Abnormal Psych.

It was time to speak with an advisor, Dr. Carlton volunteered. He looked at my transcript and told me that I only needed one more class in Spanish to major in it. I thought, what the hell? I'll just have a double major. He also thought that it would be worthwhile to get my teaching certificate, just to fall back on. I took the Education classes I needed, which also meant that I had to do practicum, my student teaching. I could do it in Psychology or Spanish. At that time, most high schools didn't offer Psychology. Spanish it was.

Dr. Carlton would serve as my University Advisor and Mrs. Claire would be my cooperating teacher at Hays CISD. Dr. Carlton was a brilliant teacher. I had him for Chicano Literature and he really inspired me. He was so freaking smart and dynamic. He was also an ordained minister or priest. You could see him riding his bike up and around campus, waving at everyone. I really wanted to be like him. He was more Chicano than I was and he was white! He was very pro-Chicano and I learned quite a bit about "my people" from him. He was so inspiring and quite entertaining. He was very influential to me.

I could not have gotten a better cooperating teacher than Mrs. Claire. She was a very cool lady. She grew up in the Rio Grande Valley, I think in Harlingen. She was very involved in the Pan American Student Forum. It's like a State Spanish Club that models itself after the Organization of American States. There's a big convention with a talent show called Noche Panamericana. She would take the Spanish Club at the school and have me go as a chaperone. It was so much fun! We stayed a couple of nights near the River Walk in San Antonio. I would later become more involved in PASF.

Sidebar: In her classroom, Mrs. Claire had a small collection of books for students to check out if they wanted. Her collection included Carlos Castaña's first book, *The Teachings of Don Juan*. It was required reading for the anthropology class called, Magic and the Occult. I bought the books for that class but had to sell them back to the bookstore when I dropped the class to take a much needed, required class. This was my opportunity to read the book. I did and was very intrigued. I ended up reading all of his books! As I finished one, I couldn't wait to read the next one. I remember going to the library in the J.C. Kellam building to check them out. I spent many hours in the afternoon up in that cool building reading. I had no a/c at the cottage. After I caught up with the books, I would wait for the new one to come out. The first new one was called *A Fire* from *Within*. After reading the first four or five books, I had my first out-of-body experience. I had floated up from where I was sleeping next to my girlfriend. I could see us both and from the open window next to me I heard a voice coming from outside. I was living out in the country at the time in a cottage. The voice was like a computer-generated language, not English, but I understood everything it was telling me. It told me not to go where I should not. I was trying to scream, but nothing would come out. I was pretty scared and started to float down towards my body. When I landed in my body, I let out a little scream. I just reached over to hold my girlfriend with my back to the window! I am a very vivid dreamer, but this was definitely not a dream. Years later, I let one of my students read it. He was the valedictorian that year and had asked me for something interesting to read. A couple of days later he brought the book back. He said he couldn't read the book. He said the words were too strong. I know what he meant.

    I was nearing the end of my student teaching and Dr. Carlton had not stopped by to observe any classes yet. Finally, on the very last day, he told me that he would be there at a certain time. Well, again he missed the class. There had been bad weather, thunderstorms. He had a flat tire and was dripping wet. He said "Se me pinchó la janta"(llanta). I felt so bad for him and he felt bad for me, for missing my observation. I think he actually caught the last ten minutes. After class, he left to speak with Mrs. Claire. They spoke for a good while, and he came back and offered me a teaching position at the University! He was the Chairman of the Department of Modern Languages at Southwest. I could not freaking believe it! He said "You'll have to go to graduate school," I said, "Sign me up!" No problem! I did have a good student teaching experience. It was fun and easy. I have found that if you speak to someone in a polite tone and manner usually, they respond positively. I now felt that I had a bit more of an idea what I wanted to do. For now, I would be a graduate student while teaching beginning Spanish 1410 and 1420, first and second semester Spanish.

On my way to visit my mother and brother in San Antonio, I was just coming from Aquarena Springs Drive towards Interstate 35. As I turned right to get in the lane to approach the southbound ramp to Interstate 35 to S.A., I'm coming up on the ramp, I look towards the horizon, its late afternoon, but still plenty of light, and I see a red fireball in the sky! It looked like one of those red fireballs that a Roman candle firework shoots out. It's just there stationary then it takes off south, in the direction of S.A. and vanishes almost immediately. I asked myself, *what was that? Was that a UFO? I think it was, it didn't look like any plane or flying machine that I've ever seen.* I kept that to myself for a while, although I did tell a few close friends.

4. Graduate School

I graduated that summer in August of '84 with my B.S.Ed. The waiting to get a contract to teach at the University was agonizing. In the meantime, I did get my Open-Water and Advanced Open-Water scuba certifications that summer. It seemed like they waited until the last minute to let me know that I was hired and would be receiving my contract. Yea! My contract would expire at the end of the semester I was teaching unless I would be rehired. After signing my contract, I attended the faculty orientation for all new teachers. There I met Julián. He was coming from UT where he had taught. He would be teaching more upper-level classes as he was working on his doctorate in Spanish. We became very good friends and spent quite a bit of time together. We attended the faculty barbeque at the University President's house. I was walking amongst some of my former and current professors! It was so cool. I loved the idea of being part of academia. Just being there where things are happening, people going places and ideas being shared. Dr. Carlton would transfer to Asunción in Paraguay where he would teach at several institutions. Dr. Pierre, a French professor would be the new chairman of the Department of Modern Languages.

I would have my own classes and be the teacher of record. My first year, I taught two classes at $300 each a month. That was $600, big money for me in those days. I eventually taught three classes which was still considered part-time. I would be making just over $1000 a month, like I said, big money.

A university professor didn't get all that much pay. My friend Julián had a friend Victor, who was an acquaintance of mine. He had a

A CHICANO SPANISH TEACHER

Ph.D. from Yale University and was only making $25,000! That's not much is it? I mean, for me it would have been, but not with a Ph.D.

Since I didn't have to pay rent with money, I would save what I earned to pay for my tuition and travel. I paid for my graduate school, but I couldn't have done it without my father who supported me for my undergraduate degree. I earned enough to survive and travel through Mexico and the Caribbean on that salary.

That fall semester I taught one day class and one night class. Oh my! I couldn't believe all of the girls! That very first class of night school I had called on this one girl, and she answered me, "Sure honey!" I couldn't believe she said that and told her not to call me that and she said, again, "Sure honey." I didn't want to make a big scene so I just blew it off and continued. My ex-girlfriend was also in that night class. We did still see each other off and on that semester.

It was the easiest job that I've ever had. It gave me an opportunity to master the grammar and all of the rules that go with it without the distractions that come with teaching in the Public schools, that would come later. Teaching was fun for me. Teaching at the University was sort of like being a celebrity on campus, albeit I was only a graduate student. I was able to go and get coffee in the faculty lounge, Pretty cool! Well, I thought it was.

That first semester in grad school I had a Psycholinguistics class with Dr. Decoy. It was a very difficult class for me. I had trouble with one of the books we had to read. I just could not understand the concepts of the book and I had a difficult time contributing in class during discussions. The other book we had was much easier for me to comprehend. It was *The Natural Approach*, by Krashen and Terrell I believe. The other book I read and re-read the chapters. I mean it was written in English, but it was still difficult.

I remember that we had to account for every minute of each class we had when working on how to do our lesson plans. It had to be very precise. I never had a school Principal need me to write lesson plans that were ever that specific. I mean, I always gave a good detail of what the objectives were and posted them on the board even when we didn't have to. The kids are ultimately responsible for their own learning and if I can help them to be better organized of course that's what I would do. They had to keep track of the objectives of the week and were also given an easy grade for just that.

We had a take home Mid-term exam for that class. I decided to go to the computer lab of the university and use a word processor rather than my typewriter. Yes, I still used one. This was 1984. I'm just about finished. I had used my notes and was writing down some stuff coming from my head. It was flowing very nicely. It was seventeen pages! I tried to be as concise as possible. My buddy and colleague, Julián, stopped by and asked me if I could let him try out his new spell checker on my paper. I guess it was on a disk. I said, No thanks, man. I'm a good speller and I'm cool. He was relentless. He kept asking and asking. Finally, I relented and allowed him to put the disk in the drive. I hadn't saved anything or printed anything yet. I wasn't hip to that type of technology just yet. He starts pressing keys and keeps pressing. I say, what's wrong ese? He said, it does not want to work. What? No mames! Don't be fucking with me ese! I told him to print a copy. He tried, but couldn't. I told him to take that disk out. He said that I would lose all of my info. No fucking way I told him! He couldn't turn off the computer either after he had called someone to ask what to do. He apologized. I was furious as I could not print it either. Much of what I had written was coming from my head and not my notes. I just knew that I wouldn't be able to reproduce the exam with the quality of that first draft. Fuck! We had to leave the computer on overnight and some computer guy would try to work it out. Shit, I couldn't believe it. That was the college version of *my dog ate my homework*!

That experience alone messed me up. It gave me an aversion or some kind of mental block when it came to technology. So long as I could just use the word processing part of the computer, and just remember to save, save, save! I just saved all of this! I think I got a C in that class. That's embarrassing. No one ever gets a C in graduate school. At least none of the people I knew. I made an A in my other class with Dr. Jones, which averaged out to a B for the semester. I could not let my GPA drop below 3.0 or I would be kicked out and not allowed to teach.

In that class with Dr. Jones, The Evolution of Spanish, I had written a research paper on indigenisms, more specifically, nahuatlisms. They are words of indigenous origins, like the language of the Mexica or Aztecs. The study was based on a list of words that 100% of the citizens of Mexico City all know. They are words like, *petate, tecolote, chicozapote, chiche, escuincle*, etc. Well, I reduced the list from a hundred words to seventy-five, just for the sake of time. I interviewed people from around South Texas for this study, including one of my former classmates who, was a teacher at Alice High School. A couple years down the road, Dr. Carlton would contact Dr. Jones for something to publish. Dr. Jones thought of my paper. Wow! I gathered what notes I had left and he managed to put it together. I did my paper in Spanish and he re-wrote it in English. And of course, he put his name on top. I didn't even care about that! If it weren't for him, I would have never gotten it published in the first place. I was now a published author before the internet! Thank you, Dr. Jones. Oh, the paper was called *The Vitality of Words of Indigenous Origin in The Spanish of South Texas: A Preliminary Study, Libertad y Marginación,* The Paraguayan Association of American Studies, 1986. I was only twenty-three years old in the fall of '84 when I wrote that. I received a certificate from Dr. Carlton and a very nice congratulatory letter stating that the paper was well received at the conference.

Confession: I allowed Dr. Jones to come out to the ranch to hunt for deer on a couple of occasions. He enjoyed coming out and just walking around and wandering in the 130 acres of the ranch. He never shot at anything. My landlords didn't allow any hunting. I had no desire to hunt, but enjoyed shooting my 30.06 every so often when they were on vacation. Dr. Jones gave me an almost new pair of boots. They fit perfect and were steel toe. I gladly accepted them and used them until I wore them out, literally! They had lasted a long time. After I got my Master's, Dr. Jones would begin living half of the year in Barcelona, where his wife was from, and the other half in San Marcos.

I think my problem as I saw it was that I had been going to school for that last three and a half years in a row. Both summer sessions included. I was getting burned out.

I spoke with Dr. Pierre about being burned out. I decided that I would take one semester off of grad school and would work on my P.A.D.I. Divemaster certification. I told him that I knew the condition for teaching was to be enrolled in grad school, but that if needed, I could still teach my classes if he allowed me to, he did. Fucking A!

I contacted John and asked him if I could do my Divemasters with him. He said, Sure! I had met John just recently on my first trip to Cozumel. He would be working as an instructor for the University out of the Dive Shop there in San Marcos. So, rather than getting the credit with the university and having to pay for the hours, John just charged me $60 to do it and that would save me mucho dinero. He was a very cool dude. I got to work the scuba table at registration when it used to be in Strahan Auditorium. What fun! We got to put all the people we wanted in his open-water and advanced open-water classes. I never had so much fun. All semester helping John out as a divemaster included filling tanks and loading up the trailer to take gear to Canyon Lake nearby. We would go to the lake via Ranch Road 12 since that is where The Dive Shop is. We would do everything in the pool at the West Campus for the first few weeks and then we would go to the lake for their open water check out dives. It was February and it was cold. We got to the lake and all of us had our own gallon of hot water to pour in our wetsuits before plunging into the fifty degree water. It was pretty freaking cold, but not for us though. We kept telling the students how great it felt. We weren't lying. Not so much for them, oh well. The water that hit our faces where we weren't covered up was cold.

John would teach Tim and I separately from the open-water classes. Tim, who was a marine biology major, I later learned, was a director of some kind at one of the Sea Worlds in Florida. One of the orcas had killed one of the trainers and I saw him on TV as he was being interviewed about the incident. He was a good guy. I never got a chance to return the book on Caribbean fish that he let me borrow. Sorry. I know that on countless occasions I lent out a book, DVD or CD and never got them back.

Since I was almost always working at the ranch where I lived, I missed my test for my Rescue Divers certification. I had some work that I needed to do right then. I never got it, but I did get my Divemasters certification. John was given permission to test out some Tekna underwater scooters at the Aqua Sports Center there at the University. It was a huge pool and I got to go all over the pool underwater! It was so much fun. It's amazing the power that it has.

Sidebar: I was In Cozumel and my girlfriend and I had drifted far from the group. One of the divers in our group had a scooter. He had it rigged it up to where he had a strap that went between his legs attached to a piece of wood that he could sit on. The scooter would pull him where it was easier for him. He saw us and grabbed my hand while I was holding my girlfriend's hand. He was pulling us both back closer to where the boat was. I was amazed at how much power those little scooters have. Those damn currents!

One year John had gotten a sponsorship with Captain Morgan's Old Spice Rum for a team at Chilympiad. It was a big chili cook-off contest. It used to be huge! It was so much fun walking around and taste testing all of the different types of chili. Our group was making rum chili, what else? I never did taste it, but I had a bunch of other groups' chili. It all of our scuba group of friends, such cool dudes. There was John, Beto, Kent, Skinny Willy, Bill of Green Parrot and others.

For Halloween that year I went with a girl I had a class with to Sixth Street in Austin. Oh my, it was so crazy. To begin with, Austin is already pretty damn weird they even have that slogan on t-shirts! We walked around checking everyone out and it is fun to see everyone all dressed up like crazies and some acting it too. We had taken a bus from campus to Sixth Street and would take one back to campus around 2 a.m. in the morning. When we returned to campus there was no one. It was deserted; it was in the middle of the night. On the way to walking the girl to her car, we walked through campus.

Confession: When we got to the quad just between Flowers Hall and the Science Building, we decide to go for it. There was no one around and we were both young and stupid, and horny, so we found a nice grassy spot next to the Science Building. Shit, what a rush! I mean, the thought of getting caught… it made it sort of extra hot and definitely exciting!

    Back at campus, I had a night class that I was teaching on Tuesdays and Thursdays. One evening I was giving a vocabulary test. I would circulate around the room and noticed a student had a piece of paper underneath his test. I quietly walked over to him and wrote a zero on his paper. He turned out to be one of my best friends, Danny. He was more upset at himself for not preparing and having to resort to cheating. He never made that mistake again. He actually made an A all by himself with no extra help from me. We were best buddies and made a couple trips backpacking into Mexico. Those stories are in my first book, *"Adventures of a Chicano Spanish Teacher, Mexico and Beyond."* I wished that I could have gone to visit him in Costa Rica when he was still alive. We had some great times, life-changing even. He would introduce me to some of his friends, like his roommates, who also made a backpacking trip with us the second time around. I sure do miss him. That summer I took an Underwater Archaeology Class with Dr. Joel Hanna of Southern Methodist University (SMU). He would come to San Marcos in the summers to teach the class. He only had one lung. I found a mastodon tooth and a bunch of flint tools there at Spring Lake. It was at what used to be Aquarena Springs, a tourist attraction with glass-bottom boats and a swimming pig. It was quite a tourist attraction. It is now part of Texas State University. We used to be able to go and do night dives. My friends and I made several. We would swim all around the springs and go into the Submarine Theater where the "mermaids" would perform. We saw turtles, spotted gar and freshwater eels. Not to mention all of the little fissures where the spring water would come up to the surface. You could see the sand on the bottom bubbling as the water made its way up. It was very cool to be able to do that. During the day when we would be digging, the glass-bottom boats would come and check us out and we would wave to the kids. We were only diving in about ten feet of crystal-clear, seventy-two degree water. We didn't need to use our fins but, we did need quite a bit of weight to keep us down. I mean a lot of weight. After about an hour, I would begin to get chilled and come up to where we had a good-sized platform where we could warm up in the sun and also hold the compressor for the airlift. One day while working underwater Dr. Shiner came up to me and did some kind of hand signals to me. I had no freaking idea what he was trying to tell me. Then he hits my mask with his open hand and yanks the regulator out of my mouth to take a hit of air! Hell, I didn't know that was what he wanted. He then ascended to the surface.

Confession: Back at the ranch, I decided to grow some pot plants. I had one in a clay pot and one out in the back by the tree line. The one in the pot matured very quickly. It was pretty with purple hairs. The one in the ground got huge. I would clip off the tops as they would grow, then they would split into two more branches. It was wider than me with my arms spread out. One of the cows had torn a big branch off. It was so big. When I decided to cut it down that one plant gave about six pounds of weed! Hell, I didn't have to buy weed for about a year and it was very good. Another year I had about six plants all by the tree line. They gave me quite a bit, but I didn't want to push it and get caught or worse, get my landlord in trouble. I just did it those two times. One weekend Julián, Dr. García and I met up in Austin and went to the Yellow Rose, a popular strip club on North Lamar. Dr. García had never been to one, so we thought it would be a good idea to go. Once there we're checking it out and I see one of my former students dancing! She had been in my class for a short period before dropping it. She seemed rather shy when she was in class. I guess she got over it and found some power in dancing so to speak. I got up to give her a donation and she did a turn and a flip where she landed with a split facing me and she says "hola!" There was another girl dancing who was a student in Julián's class at the time.

During one of the summers, I had some great students. Class started at 7:00 a.m.! What? No, really. Everyone came to class. For the final exam, I told them that we were going to play Dr. Julián's class for volleyball. I mean, they showed up every day very early to class. Would you have cut them some slack? You would think that they would be happy, ¿no? Well, most were, but these three girls. I believe they were from San Diego, Texas. They didn't like me, why? I don't know. They freakin wanted a test! A paper and pencil test. I couldn't believe it, so I gave them one. I still made them come take it at Sewell Park by the volleyball court. There were picnic tables around. The other's had fun playing against Julián's class. One of my students, this beautiful girl, she had a white bikini with Mickey Mouse on it. When she came out of the water, you could see right through it! Oh my! I had to pretend like it was nothing and tried not to stare. That was a fun summer! To make a little extra money, I used to tutor in Spanish. During one of the Summer Sessions one year, I had a student that came to me for badly needed help. The semester had already started, and if you've ever attended summer school, it goes by fast. She was desperate. She had a failing average in the 50's. She had left Spanish as her last class before graduating. It just wasn't sinking in. I charged only $10 an hour. I would meet with her at the library which was the J.C. Kellam building. They had small tutoring and conference rooms that we would use. I would meet with her every day for an hour. At the end of each session she handed me a ten dollar bill. At the end of the summer session she did graduate and pulled a B in the class. She was proud of herself and thanked me. I've actually thought that I was a better tutor than a teacher.

One semester I had a student who was a pilot. Usually on the first couple of days, I like to ask the students to tell a little about themselves so that I know who's in my class. This one kid said he was a pilot and invited me to go flying with him someday. I said sure, and gave him my number not thinking anything of it. About two weeks later or so, he calls and asks if I wanted to go and fly. I said hell yeah! We met at the SanMar Plaza and I parked by the movie marquis and we drove to Lockhart in his car. Little did I know at the time that I would teach and live there in the future. We get to the airport and he does his check on the airplane. It's a small prop plane. We get in and take off. It's so cool! We fly around a bit and he says ok, you take over. He showed me the pedals. When I bank in a direction, I push the pedal and the other direction, I push the other pedal. I drove it for a good while. We flew over San Marcos and New Braunfels, and returned to Lockhart. Oh, that was so much fun! I think I might get my pilot's license now!

One semester I was to teach at West Campus. It was a very old building. The class was on the second floor and the windows would open to a large, flat, roof. On a nice day, I asked the class to follow me. I proceeded to climb out of the window and sit on the roof. I told them to bring their books with them. They looked stunned, but soon all followed without any complaints. We had class as usual, only now, it was on the roof! Another day we went outside the building there at West Campus and there was an old amphitheater close nearby. We took a little walk over there and I had class. I was enjoying getting out of the classroom when I could.

Another semester, one of the night classes I taught had some really nice students. I usually had great students, especially since I worked the Modern Language registration table every semester. Well, that class had to do an oral presentation. I told them that we could have it at the cottage out in the country where I lived. They all agreed. I said we can all pitch in and make it a party. Immediately one of my students, Marie, asked if she could be the party chairman. I said, of course. She was Dr. Joseph's grand-daughter and she was taking my class. She was so nice and pretty, and very smart. I had made maps for everyone to get out there. It was long and winding down Lime Kiln Road. My landlords the Harris's came out to listen to the presentations and enjoy all of the good food. The students cooked fajitas with all the trimmings and we also had a keg of beer. It was so much fun. They all helped clean up before everyone had left. A few lingered a bit longer.

It was really a nice setup I had out there in the country. All the dogs were there too enjoying the show!

My friend Danny was in my class again for the second semester of Spanish. We had become good friends. We both enjoyed eating mushrooms and tripping. He had a good connection for lab-quality mushrooms. One night the students were giving oral presentations in class. During our break, Danny and I went into the bathroom there at Evans. We would be going out to a club after class and decided to eat a couple of little bad boys, small mushroom caps. We return to class and the presentations continue. There was this was girl who was having a hard time and started to stutter a bit. Oh, shit, it so hilarious and I could not laugh out loud. I glanced at Jerry and he was trying not to smile, drawing circles on his paper not raising his head to look at the girl giving the presentation. Oh, I had to tell her that it was ok to look at her paper which made it much easier for her and us!

Danny and his roommates would sometimes throw big parties. It was so much fun being there and everyone or almost everyone is tripping on mushrooms. There was much to be visually stimulated by. I had a little sort of kaleidoscope. It had a clear ball on the end of a tube that would distort everything you would look at through it, very trippy. Someone lit a lighter in front of the glass ball and wow! The visual effects were amazing and addicting. Not to mention, just watching all the people. There was always music playing and one cowboy type started dancing in front of a girl. It was so funny watching him while tripping. He started to take his shirt off and Danny jumped in right away and told him not to do that or he would have to leave. It was already getting late and the party was starting to get a little out of hand with too many people. Danny then would call San Marcos PD to come and break up the party. Everyone had to leave except the guys that lived there, Danny's girlfriend and me, the inner circle so to speak.

At another party I was feeling a bit nauseated from the mushrooms. I started sweating and I knew then that I would probably be hurling here pretty soon. I started to make my way towards the bathroom. It was very crowded and hot. The bathroom door was locked and I was getting ready to blow chow so I covered my mouth, when the door opened I rushed in. I started to hurl as I walk through the door and some came out onto some girl and she screamed. I finally got to the toilet and made a little mess. I cleaned it up and Jerry and the guys were cool about it.

One weekend on our way back from a Pink Floyd Laser-Light Show in San Antonio as we were coming into San Marcos, there was a car that was driving the wrong way in the opposite lane across the median on Interstate 35 We were tripping on mushrooms and LSD! (The show was amazing! We're all excited, saying, shit he's going to kill someone! We got off and the other car got off as well and was going in the same direction as us. As we were coming in front of the Police Station, Beto asks, should I pull in? I said, yes! We both went ran in and quickly told them what we saw. We didn't want anyone to get hurt or anything bad like that to happen. That was some crazy shit!

I had never up to now stayed up the entire night. While visiting with friends, one of them had a huge flakey rock of cocaine. It did keep me up and boy could I put away the beer! In the morning I went home and cleaned it well. I also wrote my mother a letter that I later looked at and it didn't make any sense. All the while doing the cocaine I kept asking so when is it going to kick in? Now, I'm usually an upbeat and positive person. I couldn't feel anything except for some extra energy. For sex it was terrible for me, failure to launch. Now the girls loved it, but I couldn't if I wanted to get some. For sex, MDMA or Ecstasy was a great or Qualudes, the lemon 714 were the best which I had only tried once each. I don't do that anymore and barely take a puff or two of the "weed of wisdom."

One night, Beto and I were at a club called Cherokee Cattle Company and were playing some pool. A couple of girls we knew that lived at Beto's apartment complex were there and one of them asked us to take them skinny dipping! What? I looked at Beto and he smiled, and we both said, let's go! Going to the San Marcos River would be a little too chilly and there would definitely be some "shrinkage." We decided to drive out to five mile dam. The Blanco River was much warmer than the San Marcos River. Beto drove on into the water in his jeep and parked on a small rock island. The water was shallow about four or five feet.

Confession: One of the girls was a friend of Beto's and an acquaintance of mine, I had met her a few months earlier, and she had enrolled in my class and was now one of my students and wanted some attention. What could a young man do? She was a hot little blonde who was well endowed. Oh my! I saw her off and on during that semester. Another time, I got a call one evening from Beto and he's at a bar telling me that this one girl wants to meet me and if he could bring her over. What was I to say? No? No. I told him come on over! I'm not proud of it, but it happened. Another time I had a student drive out to where I lived. My friend Julián had called while she was there. I told him in Spanish that this one woman came over for some tutoring. He said, no, she wants you! You think? He was right. We would see each other off and on for about five years. She even cleaned my house like it had never been before! There were other times, but I don't want to bore you or seem that I'm bragging. I'm a grandfather now!

Being a university employee does have its benefits. For example, the university camp, Camp Blanco near Wimberley. It is beautiful out there. I would go with one of my girlfriends who worked at the university.

Confession: She was in her late-thirties, had big boobs and she was one of my students. I didn't even know her boobs were fake until her nephew told me sometime later on. A couple of times we tripped on mushrooms out there at the camp. It was so much fun! Afterwards in San Marcos we would often go to the Green Parrot and just hang out. I really enjoyed my college experience, I was so lucky.

One semester I had a student who was in a sorority. She and her friend were in my class. She was very smart and also very attractive. She was a redhead with big blue eyes. Every year she was telling me, that her sorority invites a faculty member who is one of their teachers to a dinner banquet. She told me that she would like for me to go as her guest. She had invited me. I thought about it and later decided that it probably would not be a good idea. So I didn't go.

In graduate school, the Spanish Literature classes that I was taking required that I do research. My professor, Dra. Paez, took our class to Austin to show us where to look. We went to the University of Texas Library, specifically the Benson Collection or also known as the Latin American Collection. When I walked in there were these stacks and stacks of all kinds of books. I mean it was very intimidating. Once I figured it out, it was so awesome to have this resource!

As a graduate student, I was inducted into Phi Sigma Iota, the Modern Language Honor Society and Sigma Delta Pi, the Spanish Honor Society. In Phi Sigma Iota, we would invite and bring different speakers to the University Lecture Series. We brought Congressman J.J. "Jake" Pickle and Congresswoman Barbara Jordan. Both were excellent and inspiring speakers. Barbara Jordan, if you've never heard her speak, please look for a speech online. Oh my! She was always such an awesome speaker. Her words were so powerful, it always made my eyes water. We sure could use her now in our body politic.

When I started out teaching, all of the teaching assistants shared an office. We all had our own desks to use. This was in Flowers Hall. It was a very old building. Probably one of the first built there at the university. While I was there at Flowers, I became friends with Yolanda, a black female custodian responsible for the floor of our building. She probably was in her forties and cool as shit. She got high too! I would sometimes go and visit her and drop off some smoke. We remained friends until I left San Marcos.

The Department of Modern Languages moved into the New Evans Building where we all had our own offices. Or we shared one with one other person. Sometimes students would come in after class to check on their grades or to get some tutoring. A couple of times this woman I would see every so often, would come by my office and want to do something. I was always hesitant, but nevertheless relented. One time I was in the main office of the department with the secretary right there. The phone rings and she tells me it's for you. I get the phone and the woman starts talking dirty to me telling me what she wanted me to do to her! What the...! I nonchalantly told her that I would be available later and hung up quickly. Shit, what was she thinking?

As a teacher, I had students who approached me for a letter of recommendation. I gladly wrote quite a few. I got better at it after looking at some good examples. Usually, the ones asking for a recommendation were very smart with excellent grades and often going into medical or law school.

There was no shortage of girls, but I was ready to meet someone new to have a relationship with and not just be about the physical aspect of it, but someone to walk in life with. I am most attracted to intelligence, believe it or not. Looks are okay but, it's not what counts as much for me.

A former student of mine had stopped by my office to ask if I could tutor her. She was taking an advanced course and thought she might need some extra help. I told her sure, no problem. As she started to stop by more often I began to look forward to her coming to visit with me. I never got around to tutoring her. We just talked and had much in common and I think she kind of like me a little, not to mention she was very smart. She had a class with Dr. Galvez next door to my classroom. When I would give my class a break, she told me that Dr. Galvez would take notice and let his class out for a break. He knew that Gaye and I would talk during the break. Dr. Galvez was such a romantic. He would read us some of his poetry that he would write for his wife. He also put on the University Poetry Contest as the Sigma Delta Pi sponsor.

I had invited her to go tubing there in town, she lived in New Braunfels and she did have a boyfriend. Oh darn! I would just keep being a friend to her. After tubing I walked her to her car and shook her hand. We saw each other a couple of more times. The next time I saw her, I kissed her on the cheek at the end of the date.

This was the summer of '88 and I was taking the Language of Psychology. I had made A's on all of my papers. I got an A on my presentation of Verbal Abuse. I showed a short clip of Eddie Murphy's,

A CHICANO SPANISH TEACHER

Raw, as I was trying to make one of my points. I ended up making a C in the class and I don't know why. This meant that I would not be able to teach next semester since my GPA had dropped to 2.9. Fuck! I would have to do something different for money. I guess I could be a substitute teacher. I don't know. At least I don't have to pay money for my rent. Thank you Lordy!

After my third date with Gaye, I asked her to move in with me at the cottage. She had already broken up with her boyfriend and moved in. I didn't have any bills except for my gas card and utilities which weren't that much. She did work at a plant in New Braunfels. She had worked there for some time now. This was August.

5. Public Schools

I signed up as a substitute teacher with the San Marcos C.I.S.D. and with the Hays C.I.S.D. schools in order to have more possibilities to work. I went personally to each school where I wanted to work, so that they could put a face with the name. A little public relations never hurt. I worked pretty steadily going to schools of all levels in both San Marcos and the Hays districts. What I enjoyed the most was doing the Kindergarteners or Pre-Kindergarteners. They were so cute and they listened quite intently and attentively. After lunch, I would have them all lay on their towels or blankets, following the teacher's directions, and walk around giving them some Teddy Grahams. Of course, I would go off on all kinds of stories that I had readily available to try to capture their attention. I would get home so happy and not really tired at all. It felt so uplifting to me. I even thought that I might go and get my all-level certification so that I could teach elementary school. It was just a thought. I usually worked every day, but when I didn't want to, I would just tell them that I already had a job for that day and thanked them. That didn't happen very often.

It was the Spring of '89 I believe, that one evening as I was laying in my hammock outside by a campfire, I noticed that the usually beautiful sunset is still visible in the dark. Then I look more closely and noticed that it wasn't the usual hues of orange and dark orange on the horizon, but this was the entire sky. Not only that, but it was red purple and pinkish. What? Gaye and I watched it for quite a while. She was taking an astronomy class and the first thing that her professor asked the class that following Monday morning was, did you see it? The aurora? Gaye raised her hand and they began to have a discussion. How cool was that? I am so lucky!

I worked as a substitute teacher until October of '89 when I got a call from the Wimberley I.S.D. Superintendent. They were looking for a Spanish teacher. Apparently the one they had, had abruptly quit. He wanted me to come in for an interview as soon as possible. I told him sure, I can meet with you tomorrow. I was ready for a change and could use a steady job. The position was for Spanish 1 and Spanish 2. I drove to Wimberley via Ranch Road 12. It's a very scenic and pretty drive. I made my way to their Central Office. I met Mr. Smith and Mike O'Malley, the Principal of the High School. It was actually a Junior-Senior High School with students from grades 7 through 12. I had never heard of a school like that. It was named Susie B. Danforth, which was also called Wimberley High School. It was a small community in the scenic Hill Country. That being said, in the middle of the interview, I started to cough and sneeze. First a little then uncontrollably. They told me that the cedar must be high. I've never had that kind of reaction before. The interview went well aside from the coughing incident. I mentioned some of my travel experiences backpacking through Mexico and they seemed impressed. I did already have my Bachelor's and a Texas Teaching Certificate. I was highly qualified and was almost done with my Master's. I was quickly offered the job. They would hire me first as a long-term substitute and after a period of time, I think four or six weeks, they would offer me the full-time position. They eventually offered me the job. They told me that they would pay me $17,800 for the remainder of the year. This was 1989. It would take me ten years to break 30K teaching here in Texas!

I think this was the whitest place that I've ever been to. I think that I was the only Chicano teacher in the district, and the only one in the school where I would be working. That didn't bother me at all. They hired me to do a job and I plan to do it as well as I know how. There actually were a handful of Hispanic families there in Wimberley, but that was it at the time. There were also quite a few parents who I had an excellent rapport and got along with well, and who also took an interest in their kids learning.

I think the very first thing Mike told me was, make sure you keep the door open, especially when you are alone with a female student. *Good advice*, I thought. I had followed that advice all through my thirty some years of teaching, but also included all students period. To begin with, I never understood how a grown ass male or female teacher can be attracted to a kid. I mean, what do they have in common? Can you even have a deep conversation and about what? I have never been attracted to kids. I have been attracted to women my age or older, but not younger. I can say that a female student is pretty or say a male student is handsome, but that doesn't mean that I want to have a sexual relationship or anything like that with them, just be a good and friendly teacher and person. These teachers risk their livelihoods and reputations as educators and for what? Like I said, I don't understand. You know parents have to trust their kid's teacher and I value their trust. You don't let your kid be around just anyone.

When I started in October it was right in the middle of football season. I went to a pep rally at the gym along with everyone else. As the pep rally went on the cheerleaders began to do a very provocative dance cheer. It reminded me of the mechanical bull scene in *Urban Cowboy*, minus the mechanical bull. Oh dang! I was only twenty-nine and I had trouble looking at them. I looked around at everyone there and they were all looking and thinking it was great. It was too much. I didn't want to get a hard-on or anything. I had to avert my eyes. I couldn't believe how I felt. Some of these girls were in my classes. I remember going to one volleyball game. Their shorts almost looked like bikinis! I had a hard time watching and left early. You know I always tried to show my support for the students however I could.

At another pep rally, this one was outdoors in and around the parking lot. After the pep rally as I was walking to my car, one of the female coaches called me over where she was by her parked truck. She looked like a hell-raiser. Hey, she said. As I walked to the other side of the truck, you want a beer? I thought, "*What the fuck is she doing on*

A CHICANO SPANISH TEACHER

campus with beer?" No thanks I said. I barely started working there at the school and here she was offering me a beer? I don't smoke weed at school or go to school under the influence either. What's wrong with some people? No f'ing clue! By the way, that female coach wasn't there the following year.

Not long after I started, some of the female students that were close to the previous teacher were trying to give me a hard time about little things. They just wanted their old teacher back and I could understand that. I was bothered by it though. Then one teacher had told me, hey, you have to leave it here at school; don't take it home with you. That was great advice that allowed me to continue to teach. That along with a little weed to take the edge off!

I never really talked about my job and the everyday experiences that I had during my career. I often thought it boring for people to talk about their jobs. My job has never been my life. For some people, it's all they have and that's pretty sad. Maybe it's because of that reason, or partly so, that I decided to tell these stories once and for all.

I was teaching the uses of ser and estar, the verbs "to be" in Spanish. I had written on the entire two boards all of the rules with examples. Mike walks into the room and is shocked. He says that's too much, it'll scare them. I just like being thorough I said. I had a class of seventh graders for Spanish 1 credit. They were all top kids. One of them was a sort of genius. I think he got tested or something. He was very bright, they all were. I didn't know it at the time. I was talking to another teacher and I said, the juniors and seniors are having a little trouble understanding, but not my seventh graders. She said, oh! That's because they're all at the top of the class. From then I called them "The Doogies," after Doogie Howser from the television show at that time.

I finally had my own classroom to decorate as I saw fit. First, I brought my little cassette boombox with detachable speakers which I mounted on either side of the chalkboard, facing the students. I used this for the listening comprehension cassette tapes that came with the textbooks. I also decided to get a cheap pair of 6 X 9 speakers and make small boxes to put in and then mount them in the back of the classroom. In addition to that, I got a couple of small tweeter speakers and also made small boxes for those speakers to hang from the ceiling! I now had sextaphonic sound connected to that little boombox. I also put colorful posters of jungles scenes with all kinds of birds and animals and an underwater scene with all these pretty fish. I also had posters of Machu Picchu, a place that I have always wanted to visit and finally did. You can read about that in my first book. I tried to make my room visually appealing. I read some books that said not to put too much stuff in your rooms as they might distract students. Whatever! I would use these posters and things in my lessons, wonderful examples to use with colors and some vocabulary. I also had different maps of Mexico, Jamaica and Spain. Back then, I had these cool maps that hung from the chalkboard. They were the big old-fashioned ones that you would pull down. I really liked those maps. They were big and very detailed. I used them often in my lessons.

    Every Spring I got an invitation from Dr Galvez for the Sigma Delta Pi Annual Poetry Content at Southwest Texas State University. I had some students in mind already. I asked those that had a good pronunciation if they were at all interested. Surprisingly, they were. The two older students, one female and the other male and another younger student all went. The two older kids placed in the top three in the Non-Native category. I would see Mrs. Claire from Hays High there also. It was always so good to see her. We would have a little chat with some punch and cookies provide at the reception. She had two outstanding students who had memorized their poem and had become one with it. It was joyous to watch! That younger kid that I took said a short poem by Nezahualcoyotl. That, I do remember.

    One morning on my drive to work, as I'm turning right onto Lime Kiln road from where the Thousand Oaks entrance is, I noticed some dogs that were attacking something. There were about five or six dogs attacking a black miniature goat. Shit! I got out of my car and ran at them scaring them away. They, the dogs knew I meant business. I picked up the goat. It was bleeding badly and brought it to my car. I would drive it to my veterinarian at Springtown there in San Marcos.

A CHICANO SPANISH TEACHER

I took him in and they quickly tried to save it. Sadly, it died shortly thereafter while I was still there. A couple of days later I read in the lost and found section, Lost: pygmy goat with red collar. I called the number and told them what had happened. They thanked me for trying to save it. Another morning as I was turning from Post Road onto Aquarena Spring Drive, just as I turn there is a turtle trying to cross a very busy road in the middle of morning rush hour. I pull over and picked it up. I had it facing away from me. Mistake! It sprayed shit all over me! Fuck! I moved the turtle to safety and had to drive back to the cottage to change. My pants were all drenched. Ugh! Next time you pick up a turtle make sure it's facing toward you, with its ass pointing away.

I started to win the kids over soon enough. I was walking down the hall from the faculty lounge to my classroom. As I was coming around the corner I stopped when I overheard my name. There was this kid telling another, yeah, you have to learn in Mr. Morin's class. He doesn't let you not learn. It's kind of fun, and you know what I'm learning. I thought, *Wow! At least they're learning*, but I already knew that! I sort of took a "take no prisoners" attitude in my teaching. I was definitely stricter as a young teacher than I was when I retired. I felt that in my classes, no one had more attitude than me. I sometimes was an "in your face" teacher. I wasn't trying to scare anyone, just the opposite. I sometimes would raise my voice and yell to make my point, whatever it was. On a first day of school, I was asking everyone, What's your name? In Spanish. ¿Cómo te llamas? This one kid was so shook up he answered somewhat stuttering, Miguél, Miguél. So for the rest of the year that's what I called him, Miguél, Miguél. That wasn't his real name

At that time, around '89, Mark White was the Governor of Texas. He had all of the teachers be required to pass a test called the TECAT in order to continue being a teacher. It was a basic reading and writing test making sure that teachers are competent. Well, this really pissed off many teachers here in Texas! I mean, if they already have college degrees and teaching certificates, shouldn't they already know how to read and write? Yes, they should, but taking the test shouldn't be a big deal. Well let me tell you, teachers were worried. They were having studying sessions and group meetings for those that wanted to prepare. It made me freaking laugh! Here are all of these adult teachers worried about passing a reading and writing test. C'mon, man! If teachers couldn't pass a simple test they should not be teachers, period!

When it came time for the test, I went and sat down and opened up the test booklet. I couldn't freaking believe my eyes! It was so simple. It had questions like, where in the dictionary is, let's just say the word, "balloon." Is it between "apple and ant, or aunt and car?" Are you kidding me??? Nope, it was all like that. It took me and hour and I know that I scored 100%, although we just got a "pass or fail." If a teacher couldn't pass that test, they need not be in the classroom. I wouldn't want them for my kids' teacher that's for sure! I did hear that there were some that indeed did not pass.

When it came time for my appraisal or observation, as they called it, I was told to tell the administrator the day and the exact period and time that I wanted them to see me teach a lesson. I couldn't believe it! *I thought, isn't that kind of like cheating?* I mean, that sort of encourages mediocrity. What do you think? The PDAS instrument that they use asks for a preponderance of evidence for each section. The highest score is EE for Exceeds Expectations. My first observation I got only about two or three, but after that, I would consistently get four or five. I thought that it would be a great idea to have cameras in the classrooms to get a more accurate picture of what is taking place at any time. You know some kids act out if they don't like the teacher. They can try to sabotage the observation, putting the teacher in a negative light.

I was the Department Head, hell, I was The Department. I was the only Spanish teacher at the school and the only Chicano teacher there. The following year I would add a level 3 in Spanish. Soon, everyone wanted to take Spanish and they would have to hire more teachers that would be in a couple of years. This also meant that I was the Spanish Club Sponsor too. I would have to fundraise by selling tamales. This is what the previous teacher did. I would have the club members take orders from people in town and I would go and pick them up and distribute them. I would get them in San Antonio at *Delicious Tamales*, they were $2.35 a dozen at the time for schools. The money was used to pay memberships and attend the Pan American Student Forum (PASF) in San Antonio. They have a convention every year. That first year we just went for the day as we didn't raise too much money at all. The following year we stayed for one night and then after that we would stay two nights there in downtown San Antonio. The River Center Mall was right there. We would stay at the Crockett Hotel. We also had car washes at one of the insurance places there in Wimberley. I had the daughter of the owner in my class. The community really helped us out big time. We only accepted donations and would often raise at least $500 when we had a carwash.

I had been longing to get back to Chiapas, Mexico, specifically, the Mayan ruins of Palenque. I had already made three trips and was ready to take some students. I would only be able to take three at the most on a trip like this. We traveled through Mexico by bus and finally made it back. Later that Spring I was awarded Teacher of the Year for Secondary Teachers in the Wimberley I.S.D. I never did expect that. It always feels nice to get recognized. I would do another trip in '94 with another three students. This time we flew into Mexico City and bused the rest of the way to Chiapas. You can read about those stories in, *Adventures of a Chicano Spanish Teacher, Mexico & Beyond*.

In '92, at the PASF Sponsor's Breakfast on Sunday, it was the first one that I ever attended. I was at the table with Mrs. Claire, my cooperating teacher for my student teaching and her co-sponsor, Frankie. They were such cool ladies. The Board of Directors of PASF needed to vote for a new Program Director. Someone nominated a teacher from the valley, and then Jennifer stands up and says, I nominate Sonny Morín from Wimberley! *I was… what the f.. did you just do?* We both leave the room and when we walk back in, they all clap, I had won! I didn't even want to do it, but thought that it would be a good experience and I would be in charge of putting on the Noche Panamericana in the Lyla Cockrell Theater. It was a huge task because it was such a big show and Roel always did a good job. He was now the head guy of the whole PASF and he was a teacher at Bowie High School in Austin. He was such a character and a great guy! As were the other board members as I soon discovered. My life was about to get very, very busy.

As soon as I found out that Carlos Fuentes, one of my favorite Mexican writers, and Rigoberta Menchú, the Nobel Peace Prize winner, were speaking at a symposium in Georgetown and Southwestern University. I made arrangements to go and was so glad that I did. They spoke so beautifully, just as I thought that they would. I was able to use this as a Professional Development credit. I did read her book, *I, Rigoberta*, on one of my backpacking trips through Mexico. I really enjoyed it, but it was hard to read some of the things that she had experienced, terrible, terrible.

I was able to take a group of students to the San Antonio Museum of Modern Art to see the *Thirty Centuries of Splendor* Exhibit. It highlighted over 3000 years of Pre-Columbian art from Mexico. Art from the Olmecs to the Zapotecs, to the Maya and the Aztec's, to the Toltecs, the Totonacs, the Huicholes, oh there were so many different groups. I felt it a privilege to be there and witness this. The kids probably weren't as moved as I. It was such an excellent show.

I was always working at the ranch when I wasn't teaching. I still had to take one last Psychology course, Learning and Memory with Dr. Stevens. I would take it in the summer leaving me only with my internship to do. I did make an A which brought my GPA back up past 3.0 which cleared me to finish with my internship. Dr. Stevens, besides Dr.'s Jones and Paez would be on my committee for my internship and my final oral interview. I remember watching *Jeopardy* on television. Dr. Stevens was a contestant! I couldn't believe it! He could have won, but on final jeopardy the question was about the size of a sports field. They mention "acre" and instantly I knew that something that big could only be polo. He answered, La Crosse. What?? No way. I got it, he didn't. He was under way more pressure than I. At least he made it on the show! When I saw him on campus afterward, I said to him, Dr. Stevens, La Crosse? He said, I know, I know and was a little embarrassed. My oral with my committee went very well. I mean, they asked me about my internship. There was nothing that I didn't or couldn't answer since I did all my own research. I told them about my job and even got to show some clips of me working as a divemaster and what a dive was like. They all enjoyed it and included a VHS tape of the dive along with my paper. I had to write my paper In Spanish for my two Spanish professors and in English for Dr. Stevens. I still haven't gotten them bound.

That month of December in '90 had a lot going on. I turned thirty on the twelfth; I got married on the sixteenth, and got my Master's on the twenty-first. It was very cold that night, freezing. I remember my grandfather laughingly pointed out that there was a frozen cow patty on the back bumper of my car. Yeah, I have cows in my yard! I would say that this was the start of my "arrogant period."

I was proud of myself that I got my Master's. I had to work my butt off. They don't just give those out you know. I had attitude with the degree. I remember walking by detention one day after school. The teacher told the kid to sit down, I heard that, and told the kid; you don't have to listen to her. That was a real dick move. I shouldn't have said that. The teacher was kind of an uptight person, but I still shouldn't have said that. I later got to know her a bit better and she was an Ok person. I felt like a jerk.

Most of the teachers were quite conservative, but there were also some liberal sprinkles here and there within Special Ed, Journalism and Art. This was when you could still be friends with a conservative and be courteous. Not too much anymore these days.

One of the coaches, he was a conservative Republican and very redneck. I liked him, though. He was funny and knew about the head football coach that I had played for when I was in high school. We talked football and politics and it was no big deal, we just disagreed. I remember when Clinton won, I came in singing, "oh the times, they are a changing." He didn't like it, just like we did, but had to accept Trump's illegitimate win.

Coach had asked me if I had my Master's, a couple of years after I received it, I told him yes. He said Well, Sonny, you're a tough son-of-a-bitch! I responded tell me something that I don't know!

At the time, Ann Richard was the Governor of Texas. I thought that it would be a great idea to invite her for lunch. I sent her a letter inviting her to campus for lunch. I waited for a response. A few days later, I got called to the office, Mr. Morin, you have a call from the Governor's office! I picked up the phone and it was one of the Governor's representatives calling to thank me for the invite. She said that The Governor could not make it as her schedule was very tight at the time. I said, "its ok, please let the Governor know that she is welcomed here anytime!" Well, I thought at least I tried.

In the faculty lounge there is only one unisex bathroom, and one day I went in and there was a bloody tampon on the floor! *What the fuck?* I couldn't freaking believe it. I had to walk back out. It grossed the hell out of me! As I retreated, there was another male teacher coming in. I told him to take a look in the bathroom. He did and came out and said, those bastards! I laughed. I think he cleaned it up. But can you believe that?

One of my students, Johnny, was a sophomore. I remember he brought his Les Paul guitar to class for show and tell. It looked so cool. He was so cool. He was like one of the first wave of techies before there were techies. He would go around fixing teachers' computers for free. He should have been getting paid for that kind of work. I met up with him a few years later after he had graduated at a music store in San Marcos called Mazak's. When I got my first guitar, a Squire Strat, he gave me a couple of lessons and that was it. It was the direction that I needed. The rest was up to me and whatever *ganas* I had!

It was on either Cinco de Mayo or September 16 that I decided we would have a party. Everyone pitched in. My classroom was the first in the wing and had two windows that opened. I had a barbeque pit and made hotdogs and burgers for my classes. I even made a burger for the Superintendent as he was coming into the building. I made plates for some teachers, the ones I liked and even those that I didn't really. You gotta start somewhere. All the kids thought it was great!

Another time, we had a chapter that had vocabulary related to camping along with reflexive verbs. I loved to go camping so I brought some hammocks and took my class just past the parking lot to a grassy area that had a good spot for the hammocks and a campfire. I did my lesson outside. I had the kids bring their books and we sat around the campfire and a couple of lucky students got to lay in the hammocks. I let them bring sodas if they wanted. I'm sure everyone smelled of smoke when we went back into the building. I think they enjoyed that.

When I started teaching Spanish 3, all or most all had been my students for Spanish 1 and 2. Our school had just changed to A-B block scheduling. This meant that our classes would meet for one hour and a half every other day and on Friday's rotate classes. I thought this was a great idea. I could do more with my classes was my thinking. So, with my Spanish 3 class one year, we were doing a unit on Latin American Civilization. We all pitched in for some fajitas and chips and we all drove in students' cars to the Blanco River there in town. They had an older bridge that was way lower to the water and was closed. This is where we would have class. I even had a student in a wheelchair. She asked if she was going to be able to go and I asked, are you in my class? She said, yes. Then you get to go I said. We carried her to the back of someone's car and put her wheelchair in the back of someone's truck. We were ready to go, but there was nowhere for me to sit! I thought, wait, I'll sit on the wheelchair in the back of the truck. I get in and we go to the river! As we're driving, I'm waving at cars passing by. We take a small pit to grill the meat. As we get the fire going, they all jump off of the bridge and into the water! They swim around for a bit until it's time to eat. As we eat, we also discuss our lesson. The girl in the wheelchair didn't go swimming, she kept me company. After we got back, a couple of days later, Mr. Rankin, the principal, say's, you went in students' cars? Please don't do that again, or at least let me know ahead of time. Ok, I said, no problem. That was fun!

Also for my Spanish 3 classes I would take them to a local restaurant like the Cypress Creek Café or La Casa Blanca, one for breakfast, CCC, and the other for lunch. The kids would have to order something in Spanish for a grade. It was easy. Since their Spanish 1 days, they've been doing oral proficiency situations in class and thereby increasing their levels of communicative competency. Plus, it was fun! Who doesn't like getting out of the classroom? I know I like getting out if I can.

They had also built a yogurt shop there by the drive up to the entrance of the school. Yeppers! I would take my classes there too, and they sure did enjoy it! Not to mention that the places that I took my classes did enjoy the business as well! I never did ask permission either. I was proud that I didn't even have to write any referrals for misbehavior for quite a few years. I was a little proud of that.

I did coach baseball that first year I was there in Wimberley. We did pretty well too. Coach Nelson was the head coach and he allowed me to help out as an assistant. I didn't even get a stipend; I volunteered my time, which is usually unheard of. The following year there would be a new head coach. He brought in his crew, except for the couple of coaches that were already here and would continue coaching. I didn't coach after that baseball season until a few years later when I would go to Alaska.

I can't say enough about how great most of the kids were. I also had some great foreign exchange students from all over the world. I really liked having them in my class so that I could learn from them! They came from Mexico, Chile, Indonesia, France, Sweden, and Germany. All were highly intelligent. Amber, a student from France was very bright and quite pretty. She kept in touch after she had returned to France for a short while. She was working as a flight attendant. Another kid, Dirk, from Wimberley, was a pilot. He had been working on advancing in that industry. He was so cool. I tell you, I've met some of the best people in the world while being a teacher! I'm so lucky!

The school was doing a big fundraiser and was trying to raise $10,000. It was Wednesday and the fundraiser would end by Friday.

A CHICANO SPANISH TEACHER

They had only raised about $7,000. Mrs. Mills and Mr. Rankin had both agreed to have their heads shaved in front of the students that had raised the money. They had raised a little more. One day left and they asked me if I would shave my head. My hair was pretty long at this time. I thought, sure, I'll do it. They won't raise it. Well, they all went on a bucket brigade all over town to collect and dammit if they didn't collect it all. I went to the gym and watched the teacher and the principal get their heads shaved, and then it was my turn. I had done this one other time as a freshman in high school before spring training for football. It grows back! Everyone was happy. I don't think they liked my long hair too much anyway.

Like I said earlier, I was elected Program Director of PASF. I would attend meetings with the other board of directors. Sometimes we would fly to Dallas or have them at Bowie High School. As the Program Director my main task was putting on the show. I collected videos of the acts auditioning for a spot on the show. I received way more videos than I could accept. We always chose the acts to appear by a show of hands. It was always democratic. There were some outstanding presentations. It was actually quite fun for me.

I let the students that I took work the registration at the convention and also do all of the Master of Ceremonies introducing the different acts and schools. I didn't really like to be in the limelight, so kids respond well to other kids. I did start the convention when the lights went out; I had the sound crew play the intro of *Enter Sandman*. They had a badass sound system there at the theater and it sounded awesome! The crowd was getting pumped up and then we opened the show. It was a success. I had headphones in the sound booth directing and communicating with the crew. They were all such cool guys! I did that for two years and it was so fun. As my term expired, I didn't want to run again. There was this guy who was running for Program Director, Derek of Dallas Magnet School. He was a go getter and would eventually be the head sponsor of PASF. He would go and do that for many years. I saw him years later in 2014 when I was teaching in Alice, TX.

One of my students would write an essay for the trip we sponsored to Mexico where selected students would live with a family for a period of time. One of my students had won a place on the trip. She also attended school in Mexico. She told me that on the morning of her birthday, the boys in the village came to her window to sing her "Las Mañanitas, the Mexican Happy Birthday song. She also mentioned that she was the only one in her class who knew the story of Los Novios, Popocatepetl and Ixtaccihuatl, or Popo and Ixy for short. It's the story about the two volcanoes just outside of Mexico City. It was a legend where an Aztec warrior and Princess were in love and when she died he took her to the highest mountains where some of the good gods transformed them into volcanoes. I can't believe no Mexican students knew that story. So, the teacher asks her to tell the class the story which she does. It made her feel good to do so. She eventually became a Spanish teacher. There were three other students at this school that became Spanish teachers. I'd like to think that I influenced them just a little bit.

One thing the kids told me was that they and their parents go around wrapping people's houses in toilet paper. Yeah! It was a thing there. I thought parents do this too? Yeppers! I found that kind of odd, I'd be tempted to shoot them with a BB gun if they did that to my house! Good thing I lived way the F in the country far from here. I found that the adults here were stranger than the students. There are a lot of hills out there and you don't really know who all is out there. I heard stories of the cedar choppers, although I never knew what they meant, and devil worshipers being out there. I think they filmed *Race with the Devil* out here somewhere, I'm not sure.

One day as I drive into the school parking lot, there's this police tape all over the place and cop cars with the lights flashing. I curiously walk into the building and see all this mess. In the cafeteria, which is right there in the front part as you walk into the building had what looked like some sort of satanic symbols written in blood! *What the fuck!* There was stuff written all over the walls too. Shit, what happened? Apparently, some people set the Principal's Office on fire, as if trying to destroy some records possibly. They had broken into the Science labs and killed all of the animals they had in there, rabbits and guinea pigs and I don't know what else. They used the blood of the animals to write their garbage on the walls and floors. I thought, *I need to get the fuck out of here!* I had already been here six years and I was thinking that I need to move on.

We started looking at houses and settled on one in Martindale. I wouldn't have to work so much and so hard anymore. I wanted to teach closer to where I lived anyway. I had no idea where I would apply or what to do just yet. If I moved, I would lose my career ladder money which was just over 3K, and I had just started getting it.

One of my students had showed me a cassette tape called *Wicked Spanish*. It had a bunch of bad words. It was funny, but they were really bad. I don't know what made me, but I decided to share it with my Spanish 3 classes. This was a stupid, stupid idea. As I played the tape, I squirmed, thinking that I shouldn't be playing this. I didn't get all the way through it. It was too much to bear. I told them not to take notes, just listen. I wanted them to know some cuss words in case someone's might be talking about them. That's not a good rationalization, but it's all I had. It was really bad. I think the first phrase was "Chinga tu madre, Fuck your mother;" Nunca viajo sin mi vibrador, I never travel without my vibrator. Yeah, you're laughing now, but later it would not be a laughing matter. I knew all of the kids for three years or more, except for one new student who was in one of the classes that heard the tape. I think some of the students were talking about it and her guardian, I think it was an aunt, had overheard the conversation. She quickly got in touch with the Superintendent and they called me into the Principal's Office two days before the end of the school year.

I was in the office with the Superintendent, the Assistant Superintendent, the Principal and the Vice-Principal. They asked me if I had played this tape and they showed it to me. I said yes, embarrassingly. I told them that I was sorry and that it was very stupid of me and that I can't believe that I actually played. Mr. Smith told me that he hated when good teachers make bad decisions. I'm thinking, *yes, but I didn't kill anyone or sexually assault anyone.*

The student's guardian had gone to every parent of students that they knew had me as a teacher, even years prior. They were trying to smear me. I should have known this already. I was in an ultra-conservative school district and I should have known this was not going to flush. I had heard there was one female student that had said that I looked at her provocatively. Whatever! That's total BS. I must have had something in my eye! They suspended me on the second to the last day of school. I had to leave everything for Sheri, one of the other Spanish teachers to wrap up my classes for me. So be it! I returned to class and told them that I had to leave now. I noticed that the girl whose guardian called, had her head down on the desk with her arms around her head. I did return to school after it was out. I had quite a bit of stuff in my classroom that I would need to pick up and take home. Gaye came with me to help. I felt like I was being shunned by some teachers. I sat at a table alone. A couple of teachers did come by to say hi and if I was doing OK. Yeah, I told them. I needed to make a move anyway; I just didn't know it was going to be like this.

I had been in touch with Rogelio De La Cruz at Texas State Teachers Association (TSTA). I was just going to resign and move on. The Superintendent wasn't going to allow me to do that. They wanted to take me to court. I said, Ok let's go. I called and told Rogelio. He spoke to the Superintendent and whatever he told him, Smith would accept my resignation and I would have a clean record. Mil gracias, Rogelio. I'll remember how you helped me in my time of need. I was ready to move on.

Let me finish by saying that I was able to make contact with the three boys that I had taken on a backpacking trip through Mexico. They have all done very well, creating their own businesses. They are all family men, two of them have returned to the hamlet of Wimberley, the other lives in Maryland. I'm so freaking proud of them!

6. Junior High

It was time to move on. This would be the first time in my life that I had to go hunt for a job. I was now thirty-four and it was 1995, and every job that I've ever had, had found me up to this point. I had usually known someone who had offered me a job or like in Wimberley when they got a hold of me. I did have an interview with Bastrop I.S.D. and went in for an interview. The Hispanic woman interviewing me made sure to tell me that they were *a very conservative district, like that was a good* thing! Shit, I didn't want to hear that. I had just left a very conservative district! Well, I knew right away that I didn't want to work there. I wasn't offered the job, no problem. There weren't that many Spanish positions open. There was a Junior High position in Lockhart. Ooh, I had always heard negative stories about teaching that level of students.

I had an appointment with Mr. Charles. I came clean with him and told him what had happened at my last school. He was very sympathetic and told me that he didn't believe it was right how I got treated. I agreed. He told me the job was mine if I wanted it. I gratefully accepted. I was excited to have a job once again. The faculty at the Junior High was the best. Everyone was very helpful and supportive. I liked being a part of the team.

Mr. Charles was a very generous and no-nonsense kind of guy. He and the other Assistant Principals, Mrs. Kelley and Mr. LeBeau were very decent and fair people. I really enjoyed having them as Principals.

We laughed a lot. The students were very funny. I liked that there was much more diversity in the demographics of the student body, faculty and administration. That being said, it was the first time

I had ever been told, "Fuck You" by a student! I found out that the particular student who had cussed me out was easily re-directed. I just told them to copy what was on the overhead projector and that's all it took! Wow! I didn't even have to yell!

Now that I was teaching Junior High Spanish, I was just trying to get the students interested in the subject matter. I wasn't teaching Advanced Placement so it was much easier. Mr. Charles would allow me to take the students outside of the classroom and walk across the street to play "touch football." The kids loved it! Going outside was no big deal. I used to tell the kids that the classroom was an artificial learning environment, and that you could do some real learning outside. I've always like to take my classes outside, from the days teaching at the University to now. At the Junior High campus there are these huge old oak trees. They are big. At the front of the school, they put a table around the tree trunk so that kids could have a writing surface. We would sit around the tree and do our assignment or have our discussion.

I was trying to be a fun teacher. I had recently bought a guitar and brought it to school to show everyone. I would describe it in Spanish and then told them that they would have to pick something to bring to class to describe in Spanish. It was fun and they all usually did a very good job. I wanted it to be no big deal to speak Spanish. The more often you hear it, the more comfortable one becomes. I was always kept in mind their *affective filter*. This was the anxiety level that each student has when exposed to the language. I try to keep it as low as possible. You have to allow for a *silent period* sometimes since not all students have the same anxiety or competency level. In some it is higher and they may take a little longer to produce the spoken word. You start slow with sí or no questions. Then you could progress to this or that questions and so on.

One morning, the students came in all excited and said that they were filming a movie just down the street from the school. I just brushed them off. Then, one little kid came to me, and said, it's true Mr. Morin that they are filming. Now this was a good and honest little kid. The students had gotten him to tell me because they knew that I would believe him. Well, what do you think I did? Of course! I told them Ok, we're going to go and check it out. You all have to stay together or we're coming right back. They all agreed and we walked out of the school. We proceed to walk down the street to where the railroad tracks are. Sure enough, there was a movie set going on. In the distance I see Drew Barrymore! What? Really? She had orange hair and was walking to a car and I yell out, "Hey Drew!" She says, "Hi " to us. Wow! I later found out that she was filming *Home Fries*. That was so cool. I was wearing my Mexican poncho as it was a little cool out. That was so cool!

One weekend I called my brother Adrian in San Antonio to see if I could catch a ride with him to a funeral in Alice. It was for a lifelong family friend. He was more like family. I met Adrian in San Antonio and he drove us in his truck to Alice. Almost all the way through George West was clear of DPS patrols. There was one parked in the outskirts of town. Adrian passed them and he was driving too slowly. I told him to speed up a bit. He was frozen with fear since we, or rather, he had some weed in his jacket.

Confession: We had already smoked a half of one and we were both buzzing good. Fuck! They turned on their lights to pull us over. The officer asks if he can check the window, since it had tinting. Adrian assured him it was legal, not too dark. Then he asked if he could search for weapons. At that point, Adrian should have told him no. We didn't have any weapons. They ask us to stand behind his truck and in front of their squad car. Shit, I know they're going to find the weed. Sure enough! They do! F U C K!!! They start searching us to see if we have anything else. I told him that we didn't. Adrian says to me, hey Sonny, sorry man. I told him to forget about it. *I actually have wanted to see what the experience would be like, at least better here than Mexico.* I then ask the officer, are you going to take him to George West? He said yes, but you're going too. Shit! What you gonna do? They put some tight-ass handcuffs on me behind my back and had me sit in the back of the squad car. They took us in separate vehicles. Damn, those cuffs hurt like a mofo! I don't know why they had to put them on us? As if we were dangerous criminals.

They fingerprinted us and we got our picture taken, or rather our mug shot. It was about four o'clock in the afternoon when I was able to make a phone call. An hour had already passed. Adrian and I were in separate rooms. I called my wife Gaye and told her what was up. We would be spending the night, since the judge was gone. Hopefully he would return tomorrow, and hopefully early in the morning. We didn't get anything to eat, nothing! I was hungry as I had left Martindale early for San Antonio. Soon enough they took us to the general population. We met everyone and they were cool guys. I tried to play chess against one of them, but I couldn't concentrate and he beat me in one move! He was good, not me. The guys said that they should have fed us already by now. They all had just eaten. I'm in jail. It was a long night. Early the next morning the judge sets bail at $1000 and I would have to pay ten percent which is $100. My uncle Jesse had driven up from the valley to see if he could help us out. He had already left before we had gotten out. The bail bondsman was the owner of Garza's, a Texaco Mart at the edge of town. I actually paid for my bail with my Texaco card. An uncle of ours from George West, Hector, came to pick us up. He drove us to the car pound to get Adrian's truck. We thanked him and had missed the funeral. I really wanted to be there. Adrian still had some roaches in his ashtray that we soon smoked as soon as we got out of George West. My mother would be pissed at us for having missed the funeral, but eventually forgave us. What a speed trap that place was, probably still is.

That was the only time that I have ever been arrested. It was for possession of marijuana. Since it was my brother's, he took the blame. The husband of one of my mother's cousin's Marie, was a lawyer and would take our case. At our court date he couldn't make it, so he called the judge to tell him that my brother was taking the blame since it was his weed. The judge dismissed my case, but I still have an arrest record and had not bothered to get it expunged.

Confession: From that point on I made sure that every time that I drove through George West, I would light up a joint and smoke it all the way through town. Every single time and there were plenty! And luckily I never got caught.

Sidebar: One time traveling from the valley back to Alice, our car still smelled of weed. It was from the doobie I had smoked earlier as we left Mercedes. When we arrived at the Border Patrol Checkpoint in Sarita, they had us get out of the car. It was Lydia and I, my daughter, and two grandchildren. I didn't have any weed, but the dog had to make sure. I had a little white tube that these small cigars came in. They're excellent for transporting a joint, which I had. It was in the car and the officer said that it had marijuana residue and threw it away for me, thank you Sir.

I was able to confide in the Home Economics teacher as to what had happened. I'm just lucky that I was able to make it to school on Monday morning. What a weekend!

Teaching in the Junior High was not bad at all. I actually enjoyed it. The following year I added Spanish 1 to eighth graders which would now be a full year class. I would still have some seventh grade classes that were only a semester long. At least with Spanish 1 they could receive a high school credit and at least they would be able to hold their own at the next level in high school.

I had received a note from a parent of one of my male students. The kid wasn't failing my class or anything. He was a nice kid who behaved well so I wasn't sure what it was about. I think he may have been having some trouble in some of his other classes. I think his mother just wanted to touch base with all of his teachers. I wish more parents would take more of an interest in their kid's education. She comes by my classroom after school and when I opened the door to greet her and let her in, I was shocked. Oh my! She was so beautiful! Really beautiful. I mean, she looked like a human doll. The kid was cute and now I know where he got it from. I had to be cool which I was. I don't like to say I'm cool. I'm from the school that says, only other people can call me cool, not myself because then it is negated.

For some reason that I can't remember now, I was really mad with Gaye. I was in San Marcos on my way home, I pulled into Mazak Music. They sold guitars and amps. As I was looking at the guitars, Gaye said, you know we can afford one, I said, I know. You don't have to tell me that. So, I bought a black Squire Standard Stratocaster with a white pick guard and a small 15 watt amp. I couldn't believe I finally bought a guitar! I saw one of my former students, Johnny, and asked him to come by to give me a lesson which he did. He gave me the direction that I needed. I would get myself a Fender American Standard Strat within a few months! It was Olympic white with a maple fingerboard, beautiful! I learned the *Star Spangled Banner* in a month, just in time to play it for the Talent Show that year!

One day as I was walking by a classroom, I heard some guitar playing and it sounded good. I took a peak and it was one of my students, Brian. He was playing *Outshined* by Soundgarden. I had him show me. It was easy and it sounded good. Tony was there too. He told me that I should go and check them out, to hear them play. I was now in charge of the Talent Show and told them to play The Beautiful People by Marilyn Manson and they agreed. I went to see them at Tony's house. He had a room in the backyard where they had all of their gear set up. They played it for me and I was freaking blown away! It sounded so good. I was like dang! They said they couldn't find a singer. What? No singer? You guys need a singer I told them. People need to hear you guys I said! I thought for a minute, now I'm no singer, but these guys need to be heard and the Talent Show is this Friday! I told them that I would sing the freaking song. They didn't have anyone else and I really didn't want to do it but, they really needed to be heard so that's why I decided to do it.

We rehearsed and rehearsed. It was hard remembering the lyrics and I had to change a couple of words since I would be singing the song at a Junior High School. When it came time for the show Tony started in with the drums then Brian came in with the guitar, then Chip on bass. It sounded freaking good. I tried to imitate a bit the vocal part. At the end of the song, I lost my place and messed it up for the guys to nail the ending. That was all me. The band sounded awesome! They then played an instrumental of the song *Blind*, by Korn. I knew then that these guys could go somewhere with music.

I would put together another band the following year and start a guitar club. Everyone wanted to be a part of it. Well not everyone, but there were quite a few kids. They would come in after school and just talk guitar. Hell, I was barely learning myself. We talked about how to change strings and how to play different riffs and stuff.

Mr. Charles was no longer at the high school and the Junior High has already had a few different Principals. I kept getting more and more students as well. The electives like Spanish, Art, and P.E. were dumping grounds for students. I already had 175 students and I didn't see my situation changing anytime soon. I decided that I would go to the high school and talk to Mr. Charles and or the counselors to see if I could teach an AP class in Spanish as it wasn't being offered. When I got to the high school, I spoke with one of the counselor's there and she told me that they had the "status quo" there at the school. I'm thinking, *what the fuck does that mean, and what are you saying?* I know what it means. After hearing that, I knew then, that my days here were coming to an end. I don't know when or how, but I'm going to start looking. That same counselor I would see in a couple of years as an Assistant Principal at a different high school.

My grandmother passed away in May. She had been in a nursing home for some time now. She had to have her legs amputated below the knee several years prior. I went to Alice for her funeral and drove back later that evening. There was a spectacular lightning storm we kept watching all the way back to Martindale. When I woke up in the morning and went outside, I noticed that our car was in the backyard and the gate was shut and still had a padlock on it. What the....? I noticed that the fence looked like it had been moved a little but was still shut. How did the car get into the backyard is what I want to know? All I can think of is that due to the lightning storm, perhaps somehow, the car ignited and pushed its way through the fence. I'm still confused, it was a mystery. I take comfort that my grandmother went straight to the Lord. They say that if it rains when a person is buried, that they go straight to Heaven. Who knows?

I had always wanted to go to Alaska. I decided to start looking into teaching there. I got in touch with the Alaska Teacher Placement people online in February of '99. There were a few openings, but there were some. I decided that I needed to attend the big Job Fair in Anchorage that they would have in April. I contacted my cousin in Anchorage, Sammy, to ask if I could stay there while at the Job Fair. No problem. The counselor at the Junior High where I worked, told me that I wasn't going to go to Alaska. I thought, *who the fuck are you to tell me that?* I don't guess she knew that I had convictions and a mind of my own.

I did go to the Job Fair and had packets already made for those districts that I was interested in. None were very promising. I even had to take a Math test for the Mat-Su district before they would even talk to me. I wasn't signing up to teach Math. Why did I need a math test? I would have to take the **PRAXIS 1 EXAM** to get my Alaska Teaching Certificate. On my last day of the Job Fair, I met the Assistant Principal from Homer High School in Homer, Alaska. I did have my portfolio with me. I was walking with him on his way out to the airport as he needed to get back. He asked if he could take back my portfolio with him to Homer to show to his principal. I reluctantly agreed, but it's probably a good thing. I think it got me hired!

I would return back to Texas to finish out the school year and hope for something good to happen. Unfortunately, when I was there in Anchorage the last few days of April of 1999, the Columbine shooting had occurred in Colorado. Students and teachers were now being gunned down by other students! This is crazy! Since then, now in 2022 there have been hundreds of school shootings. The coward Republican politicians protect the gun manufacturers and donations from them, rather than the kids. We have to vote every single one of them out. This is not America, but I'm afraid that it already is. We can change this by putting people who you know will do something about it. Forget about thinking the fascist Trump MAGA's will do anything different, they let didn't renew the assault weapons ban when it expired and this is what we have now. Vote Blue for positive change!

I was able to put a couple of bands together. We had the same drummer. I had shown one of my students a song and they played it well. We were playing a Tool song and about mid-song the kid forgets the words and we keep playing until close to the end when he remembers the lyrics. He was pretty embarrassed. He said it was my fault that I messed up. No matter, I didn't have anything to prove. One of our Math teacher's boyfriend had a band, Shovelnose, and I invited them to play at the Talent Show. They gladly accepted and jammed out. That might be the only time some of those kids might ever get to see a live band like that. It is a very poor district. School let out and I had a phone interview to do with Rick Peterson, Principal of Homer High. He called and I had a whole committee sit in on the phone interview. There was a parent, who was from Mexico and had a Mexican restaurant there in Homer who would speak in Spanish to me as part of the interview. Mr. Patton said that they also needed a football coach. I told him I was their man since I could coach football and baseball if needed. I thought the interview had gone well. A few minutes later, I got another call from Mr. Peterson offering me the position of Spanish teacher and football coach. Yes, I accept! Another chapter begins! I then went to the Superintendent to deliver my resignation. It was a great opportunity for me to have taught here having made so many friends. The kids were great as were my colleagues and it was a great experience teaching at this level.

7. Teaching in Alaska

Moving is never easy, especially when you have to do it yourself. It helps to get rid of as much as possible. I gave my living sectional sofa to my brother and my mother had a love seat that she wanted to get rid of so I took it. I had not been feeling well and had a fever. Adrian and I put the love seat in his pickup and drove from S.A. back to Martindale on Loop 1604. Back then it was only a two lane and very, very, busy road. We are traveling on it and there's a blowout on the driver's side front tire. Fuck! We pull over off to the side of the road and there is no shoulder. Adrian pulls off as much as he can without rolling the truck down the hill. In the meantime, the 5 o'clock traffic is in full throttle! I have a fever and am not feeling good and Adrian can't help me because he has a cast on his arm and wrist. Shit! Ok, no problem. I put on the emergency brake and flashers, and then got the jack and lug wrench to remove the tire. I told Adrian, stand there by the back of the truck and just keep an eye out for cars coming at us. I was not more than four feet away from all of the cars. It was nerve wracking. As I removed the first lug nut, I noticed that the rest of them were rounded! What the fuck Adrian! I tried to stay calm, and then I began to say a prayer to God for some help. Then I prayed to my grandfather, Papo, who was a mechanic. I asked him to help me get these motherfucking lug nuts off! I put the lug wrench back on the next one, even though it was rounded as they all were. I just worked it and worked it and prayed until I finally got it off. Then the next one, the same, working it and praying until finally I got them all off! Thank you Lord!

A CHICANO SPANISH TEACHER

I gave my ping-pong table to one of my neighbors and sold my trailer or what was left of it to another neighbor for $75. It made for a good project. It was the one that I lived in when I first moved to San Marcos. It starts by boxing up stuff and deciding what it is that you can get rid of, maybe a yard sale or something to help getting rid of some things. I had successfully gotten a job by doing my research online. It was now my then wife's turn to get a job. There was a mental health facility there in Homer that flew her in for an interview. While she was there, she had to find a place for us to stay. She drove around with a local realtor showing her properties. She settled on a two-bedroom house out by Fritz Creek which was down on East End Road about twelve or thirteen miles from town. It was out in the country. She was able to secure a place for us and the hard part was to drive all the way up to Homer. It would be 4,376 miles from Martindale, Texas to Homer, Alaska!

We had to pack and sell our house, then make the drive. Our house sold in two weeks! Everything kind of just fell into place, nice. My father, my mother and Carlos, my brother Adrian, my best friend Lou and the Jingles all came to help us load up the U-Haul truck. The Jingle's were a couple who taught Biology at the Junior High. Mr. Jingle had given me a piece of King Salmon and Halibut, both of which were delicious. Anyway, we rented a twenty-four-foot truck; it would cost us just over $3K. They gave us fifteen days to return it to the U-Haul place there in Homer, on the Spit.

I would be driving the truck and my then wife Gaye, would be driving our new Subaru Forester. We would be communicating with walkie-talkies while on the road. She would be transporting our three cats, Rusty, a big grey tabby, Chica, a smaller tortoiseshell tabby, Mickey a big fluffy red tabby and Alex and Max, our two Dalmatian-Labs. What an endeavor it was about to be. We got tranquilizers from our Vet to help the dogs and cats relax during the long, long drive. Alex, we also called him Grande, didn't like going to poo anywhere but his own backyard.

Sidebar: In just the previous fall, we had to evacuate our neighborhood in Martindale because of threat of the San Marcos River flooding. We were already in a hotel, but Alex wouldn't go. So, I drive him back home to the backyard in a freaking storm so that he can poo! The things we do for our canine and feline family members!

The following year we had another system come in from Mexico and it brought much rain. Like nine inches in a couple of hours. I had my two dogs and three cats. A fire truck had come by our subdivision to evacuate people. I asked if we could bring our animals and they said, no. That was at about 10:00 in the evening. At about three o'clock in the morning the fire truck came by again. They told us that it was going to be rooftops soon. I had my doubts. I asked if we could bring our animals, they answered, yes! We packed our two cats, Rusty and Chica together in a big crate, Mickey in another crate and then Alex and Max on leashes. They were all so well behaved. We all got in the fire truck. Alex and Max were Dalmatian-Lab mixes, looked perfect. It was raining and we were all wet. The truck took us across the creek and from there we boarded a school bus that took us to the school gym in Luling, fifteen miles away. At the gym there were no cats crying out or dogs barking. I think they all knew that it was a situation and had to be cool. The bus took us all back to the subdivision the following morning. It didn't get to rooftops only. The water didn't even come in our house. I had all of our electronics up high just in case. Our neighbor Freddy didn't leave. He said they tried to get him to, but he refused to go. I asked Dr. Dan, the vet, if it would be a problem by not having a movement. He said, no, he'll go when he has to. I said Thanks and Ok.

On our first leg to Wichita, Kansas, Alex didn't go. On the next leg to Fort Collins, Colorado it was still nope. The dogs and cats were very well behaved. We had started out with Rusty and Chica sharing a crate and Mickey had his own. Before we got to Fort Collins back in Colorado, I had given Rusty a tranquilizer and he just plopped down on Chica. She was raising all kinds of hell! We had to get Chica her own crate at a pet store there in Fort Collins. When we got to a rest area in Montana, under the big sky, he finally went. Ok we got that over with. Crossing the mountains there in Montana was something else. When I knew there was a big incline, I had to pick up speed coming down the one I had just gone up. That and applying my brakes on the way down so that I wouldn't freaking crash! When I finally crossed the mountains, we drove into St. Mary's, Montana. I had to get some gas as we would be crossing over into Canada. A gentleman who was getting gas said, hey your engine is smoking! I said, No, it's my brakes. I had to use them quite a bit coming down that mountain!

The Canadian border was in the middle of nowhere! We went in and I had read in my research that sometimes they can make you take out everything from the truck so that they can make sure we aren't bringing in any contraband. I answered all of their questions and then he asked, have you ever been arrested? I sighed, and said, yes. I told him the story and they let us go on. They made sure that we had enough money and credit cards to make it through to Alaska. I also let them know that I had two rifles, 30.06 and a .22, a 20-gauge shotgun, and a .22 pistol. No problem, we were on our way.

We spent our first night at the Holiday Inn in Red Deer, Alberta. There I was wearing my San Antonio Spurs cap that my brother bought me. They had just won the NBA Championship earlier that year. The clerk recognized the cap and said, Yeah! I'm from San Antonio! Cool, I said. On the way to Red Deer, there were mustard seed fields on both sides of the highway. It was very yellow and pretty to see. We would pull over after driving an hour or two to let the dogs out to do their business and we would set up the litter box in the car for the cats. I would then clean out the litter so that there would be no poo in the car. We had a good rhythm going and the animals already knew the drill. The car was already smelling pretty ripe, like a barn. In the cab of the truck, I had set up my cassette player with two backpacks full of cassettes. I listened to one whole bag, then the other. On one leg, I got Rusty, my cat, in the cab with me. I had his crate on the floorboard. I stuck my finger in the door to rub him, and the little fucker bit me hard and drew blood! He was such a mellow cat and that was very odd for him to do. We were traveling across the continent though. It's not every day you do that. The next day we were driving through Calgary. It was hopping. There was quite a bit of traffic on the freeways. We pulled off into a mall parking lot to assess what we were going to do next. In the parking lot there were hardly any cars. I started to back up slowly. I assumed that there weren't any cars, but I wasn't sure. I slowly backed up into the back of a car! Fuck! Fuck! Fuck! Shit, I was pissed at myself. I walk to a Chinese restaurant there across the parking lot to see if it was someone's car there at the restaurant. An Asian man comes out. He's pissed too. Shit! He kept saying, my deductible my deductible! It was not a very big dent at all. I asked him, will you take $300 cash? He sure did. I didn't want to have to negotiate. I just wanted to get the hell out of there with no troubles!

We bypassed Edmonton, another huge city. We stayed at Valley View and then went on to camp out. We had been driving for some time when we had to stop to allow the herd of thousands of caribou crossing the highway. It was quite a sight to see. We pulled into the campground around 11:00 P.M. and there was still enough light to set up our tent and get ready for a cold night. We let the cats out for a bit. It was a wide-open campground in bear territory, but not too many campers. Rusty, climbed up into the back of the truck. He went quite far in. Gaye had to climb up in there going over chairs and stuff and found him lying on some rolls of paper towels. She got him out and we all settled in together for a cold night. It was truly an amazing drive. The natural beauty of the country is breath-taking! I will be thankful for having the opportunity to do this. I was somewhere in British Columbia when on July 28 it started to snow. At the gas station where I was, I asked the guy, is this normal? He said, no.

We were in the Yukon Territory down the road from Whitehorse. The hotel we stayed at had a Chinese restaurant there. It was pretty good. I tried to get some channels on the TV, but I could only get PBS to come in clear and guess what was on? Austin City Limits! Yes, in the Yukon Territory I'm watching ACL! Wow! Small world no? We get to bed and get up early. We hit the road at 3:00 A.M.! We wanted to cover some ground. We go by Whitehorse and on our way out of the Yukon we had a picnic on the shores of Lake Kluane. It was a glacier fed lake and had turquoise looking water. The shore was made of smooth flattened rocks. I kept an eye out for bears, since we were in their territory. On the way back to Texas, I did see a mother bear and cub going in the opposite direction as I was. I couldn't stop to video it. We ate, rested, and made our way to Tok, Alaska. We finally made it! We drove around sixteen hours! We would stay the night in Tok. We drove the next day to Anchorage. On the way coming down from Tok you could see St. Elias, the mountain. It looked so cool. I kept looking at it in my rearview mirror. I couldn't believe that I was there. It was so freaking cool! Further on down the road, a rock struck the Subaru's windshield and cracked it. Shit. Somewhere on the way we pulled into a country store and called our Allstate agent back in San Marcos. He made arrangements for us to get it fixed once in Anchorage. The woman at the store said that a brown bear had come around a couple of days earlier. I'm in bear country! We quickly made our way to Anchorage and I stopped by my Cousin Sonny's house to say hello after getting the windshield fixed. We head for the Kenai Peninsula and Homer!

On the way to Homer, we drove the Turnagain Arm with a beautiful view of Cook Inlet and the mountains. Turning to go to the Kenai Peninsula, there was a tall green mountain where we turned. It was majestic! Further on down, we stopped in Soldotna where the Central Office for the Kenai Peninsula Borough School District was located. I found it easily and went in to get all of my paperwork and to turn in some of my own. The woman that was in charge was named Brynn. When I went into her office to speak to her, I was taken aback by how beautiful she was! I mean, freaking gorgeous. I can only remember one other time when I felt like that, almost dumbfounded. I had to try to be cool and nonchalant. She was so friendly and helpful and I thanked her and was on my way to Homer! Coming through Soldotna, it was a good-sized little city with the turquoise blue water of the Kenai River flowing through it. People from Homer would go to Soldotna to do most of their shopping since it was a little cheaper. The grocery store in Homer was a little expensive.

    I was becoming familiar with some of the names of places, like Nikinski and Kalifornsky and Sterling. We had just passed Anchor Point and were headed into Homer. Oh my! Coming over the hill I could see Kachemak Bay and the glaciers! Wow! I had never seen beauty like that before! It's truly jaw-dropping and I would be living here! I can't believe it!

    I pulled into the Eagle grocery store there in Homer to call Head Coach Daryl to let him know that I had made it. He said that he would see me tomorrow at school for the first day of football practice. No rest for the weary! We still had to drive to our house to begin the process of unpacking, but first we needed to go by Bay Realty to pick up the house key. We would be living out down East End Road passed Fritz Creek on Greenville. We were going up in elevation as we are on a ridge. I was told that we have two extra months of winter living up here because of the altitude, one month early and one month longer. We finally made it to where home would be for the next school year. It was on McNeil Canyon and just down the road from McNeil Elementary School.

    The first thing I noticed about the house was that it had a flat roof. Don't people know that it snows here! I knew that I would probably be shoveling it to prevent a cave in. The grass was tall all around the house. That would have to wait. Gaye and I unloaded what we could before it got dark. We got the bed out and whatever else we could handle. I would need some help with some of the other stuff, like the refrigerator. We had a flight of stairs to go up to get to the house. I know that the cats and dogs were relieved that we finally made it. They were tired of the road. They all behaved so well.

    One thing that I would have to get used to was going to town to get my drinking water. Oh, I had water in the house, I just couldn't drink it. It was sulfur water. We could use it to shower and do laundry, we just couldn't drink it. You could smell it too. It turned our white linens a yellowish-dingy color. We would have to go to the Eagle

A CHICANO SPANISH TEACHER

Grocery store to get the water for free. They had a hose outside by the store we would use. Quite a few people had to get their drinking water there. People in town had good water, but not where I lived out there on the ridge.

I was tired and also running a fever. I still had to go in. It would be non-stop for a good while. We already had a scrimmage the following weekend! I get to the school and go to the Coach's Office and meet everyone including Rick, the Principal. He was such an easy-going guy. He played guitar too! I would be seeing him later on. I would still have to go back to Soldotna for my New Teacher Orientation in the next few days. At school in the locker room, I got some new coaches clothing. I usually hate coach's clothes, but these looked pretty cool and a cap too. As I looked around at the boy's getting their gear together, I noticed that most don't know that there are pockets in the pants to put the pads in! Oh my! They don't play Junior High football. They all start as freshmen on the C-Team. That's what they call it. I would be coaching the Junior Varsity and C-Teams. I would also help the varsity up in the press boxes during the games. There was six of us coaches all together coaching football. There were a couple of other coaches that came out periodically to help out as well during practice. I do notice the size of these kids. They were freaking huge! I'm thinking, *Shit! We're going to wipe everyone out!* Famous last thoughts! I was able to roundup some football players to help me unload some stuff. They came out that first afternoon and knocked it out. ¡Muchas gracias!

The next day I went to my new teacher orientation meetings at the Central Office building. I was hoping to say hi to Brynn! Our teacher development was Critical Incident Training. We had to prepare for earthquakes, tsunamis and volcanoes! What the...! No shit, really. This stuff does happen here and you have to be ready to respond. I would like to know what to do, for sure no question. I go through that and meet some of the other new teachers. There was a nice young woman from New Hampshire who would be teaching Chemistry. I think that I would be the only Chicano there on the faculty. I didn't think anything of it. We also had our big district meeting. Teachers came from all over the district. It was over twenty-five thousand square miles big! I got to meet all of the foreign language teachers from throughout the district. I met a teacher from Seldovia, a little village across the bay who needed some books. I told her that I would send her any extras that I had. There were teachers from Russian villages like Nikolaevsk. I'm not sure if I spelled that correctly. In order to get my Alaska Teaching Certificate, I have to take two classes on culture. I was looking forward to taking the classes. They give new teachers a couple of years of leeway to complete the courses. The PRAXIS 1 Exam that I had taken earlier for my certification, came back one point short in Math. Fuck! I would have to take it again next month. They made sure to tell me that at Central. There were so many teachers when we all met in the giant auditorium there at Kenai High School. I got to meet some of the other coaches like Mike and Rosco. I usually don't carry cash on me and didn't have any for lunch. I don't know what I was thinking. Mike let me borrow ten dollars. He was a real cool guy. He had a huge Huskie that he would take around in the back of his truck.

When the Superintendent addressed all of the teachers at our district meeting, she spoke to us in such a respectful and generous way. She said how the district was so lucky to have such hard-working and dedicated teachers working in our district. I just wanted to shake her hand! I did eventually when she was coming towards where me and my group were. I thanked her for the opportunity to work here in the Kenai Peninsula Borough School District. She thanked me for coming to teach here from Texas. It was such a nice change to be valued as a teacher.

    Homer was a small town with great views, of the bay, the glaciers and the mountains. It's a quaint little town with more Subaru's than I have ever seen in one place. It was a dog town as well. In pretty much every parking lot you go to for whatever reason, there is mostly several canines waiting for their people to do their business. I liked that. I also took my dogs everywhere with me when I went into town.

A CHICANO SPANISH TEACHER

That first week of school was interesting. I just wanted to know who these kids in my classes were. I had already met some of them who were on the football team. It was mostly a white population with a sprinkle of Hispanics and Native Americans. Rick, the Principal, told me that the students here at Homer take their learning seriously. Excellent! I said. I had so many questions that I wanted to ask them and did. One of the first questions that they asked me was, "Have you ever had any salmon? I answered, yeah. Then, they asked well, what kind was it? And I answered; I think it was pink salmon. Then, a whole bunch of them started saying, Ooh, ooh, that's dog food! I told them, fried up in a patty then put in a tortilla, well, they're pretty good like that, I said. The following day, no kidding, as many of them walked into class by my desk, they left me about twenty-five or so packs of vacuum-sealed smoked king salmon. They were right! No freaking comparison! I munched on those for a while.

After the first week in September, I asked the classes, "Hey, What's next week? No response, no clue. I said, September16 ring any bells? Nothing! I said, Mexican Independence Day! We're going to have a party. I'll pass around a sign-up sheet to let others know what they're bringing. If you can't bring anything, no problem. They all looked at me asked, we can have a party? I said, yes! I don't think they had any parties of any kind at school. I guess they had never had a Chicano Spanish teacher before. When it came time for the party, Wow! I had never seen so many different kinds of good foods. They brought smoked salmon, smoked halibut, caribou jerky, King crab and all kinds of other stuff. I sent out plates to the secretaries and different teachers. I try to share the goodness! I had a kid, Skylar, who made some of the best hot sauce. It's just how I like it. It's kind of like the hot sauce from Dairy Burger in Alice, TX! His dad worked as a crab fisherman. One day he brought me a grocery plastic sack full of King Crab legs! One of the teachers said, "Hey, that's about forty-five dollars of crab. Another time, he brought me a Tupperware box of shredded King Crab with half a stick of butter on top! Can you believe that? He was such a cool kid. I tell you, I've met some of the coolest people around being a Spanish teacher. I also had a student who brought me her leftover smoked halibut she had for supper the night before. She said she thought about me. It was very good!

On the way to our scrimmage in Seward, I was traveling with Coach Bailey in his pick-up truck. I considered him my mentor and I just wanted to pick his brain. I had so many questions. I needed to learn a lot very quickly. As we were driving along, there was a stream running parallel to the road. As I looked more closely, I saw the red sockeye salmon all along! I asked the Coach, hey are those salmon? Yes Sir! Prior to leaving earlier in the morning, Mickey, our cat, had hunted and killed a rabbit and left it on the back deck. I cleaned it up, but there was still some blood left on it. I asked the coach if there were bears out where we lived. He lived about a mile down the road from me. He said, Yes Sir! *Shit!* I thought. When we got to Soldotna at the Fred Dreyer's store, I called Gaye to tell her to clean up the blood on the deck. I didn't want to attract any bears. After learning that, we decided to keep our trash inside of the house in a little room that had a door to the back.

At one of our first faculty meetings at Homer High, one of the new teachers, the one from New Hampshire, asked Rick, "Do we have casual Friday's here? And he answered, wear clothes. Then she asked, can we wear jeans on Friday's? He answered wear clothes. I thought it was funny. They were pretty laid back as far as faculty dress code. Back in Lockhart, we had a dress code. They felt clothes make a person. Not here, thank you Lord! I still liked to wear a tie every now and then. I never saw the auto tech teacher in anything but his Carhart overalls. Besides that, I had never been spoken to like Rick and the other Administrators did to me. They actually wanted to know what I thought about whatever we were discussing in our faculty meetings. They actually gave a damn! They listened attentively and didn't feel like their authority was being threatened by that, unlike everywhere else that I've taught, Texas.

Sidebar: One thing different here in Alaska as far as teaching goes, the Administration encourages the students to call their teachers by their first names. They wanted the students to feel comfortable enough to do so. I don't mind them calling me Sonny, as they did in graduate school. They preferred to call me Coach anyway. I think that would be a hard pill to swallow for some teachers, especially here in Texas.

Most teachers here were quite friendly and helpful. However, when the secretary was doing a training for all of the new hires, we were all standing around the copier, when another teacher walks in and gets pissed because she has to wait a bit to make her copies. She says in front of everyone, "Oh a bunch of twits" and storms off. I think her name was Betty, she taught Psychology and was pretty stuck on herself thinking she was all that! Not so! She was also on the board of the Mental Health place where Gaye worked, which I'm sure inflated her head even more!

At the Seward scrimmage I wore my rubber boots since the sidelines were very wet and muddy. At the C-team scrimmage, it's sort of like a controlled scrimmage even at real games. We as coaches could go on the field and tell them in the huddle what to run. It seemed rather odd to me. Back in Texas, we couldn't go on the field like that during the game, perhaps only at a scrimmage but certainly not a regular season game. After the first football game, Coach Daryl came to me and asked, what are active backers? I responded, what are you talking about? He said. Exactly! During the Varsity game I was on the field helping out there. Sam was in the press box reporting to Coach Daryl. Sam was a little excitable. Daryl had no idea what he was telling him and wanted me in the press box from then on. Sam did invite Gaye and I out to his house for dinner one evening. It was between Homer and Soldotna, probably about twenty miles or so from Homer. He had a very nice family and he showed me the bed frame he built out of logs. Oh wow! It was huge! I sure would hate to have to move it. When we headed back it was already dark and the wind was blowing some snow across the road. It was light. It looked pretty cool. As we were driving, I saw a moose by the edge of the road. Good thing. They are so hard to see at night.

At home I had managed to cut the weeds around the house. I had to use my weed eater first as the weeds were pretty tall and I couldn't get my lawnmower in to cut them. As I cut the tall weeds there was one that had a flowery top with a long stem. My dogs Alex and Max laid down on the parts that I had already cut. They had gotten some burns from the grass. I put some tea tree oil on their blisters and it cleared them up right away. I told Coach Bailey about what had happened. He said, oh, you got into some Pushkin. Apparently, it's edible when it's young. I cleared about a ten-yard circumference around the house. At the ground level under the house was storage area. It was lined on the ground with thick heavy plastic. I was able to store quite a bit of stuff underneath. On the other side of the house was an oil storage tank for my Toyo heater that was in the house. It was about a quarter full and had someone come out to fill it up. It cost about $125 back then in 1999. The front of the house had a small stream running through it. There was a culvert to allow it to flow downward. You could hear it flowing in the winter time under the snow even though you couldn't see it. There was a wooden walkway to use to get across the front of the yard closer to the house in high snow.

The first time it snowed several inches sometime in November, I shoveled it out of my driveway. I had a snow shovel and a big snow scooper. It was exhilarating! I was excited about it and let the kids know what fun it was and they were like; you have got to be kidding me? I insisted that it was indeed fun for me as it was a novelty. I soon realized that it was hard work. Good thing Coach Bailey had a snow plow business and a couple of his customers lived in my neck of the woods. After he plowed their driveways, he came and did mine. He charged $1.00 per minute, but he never charged me. I told him that I would pay him. He told me that it really didn't take that long, so it was no problem. Cool. Before I left back to Texas, I gave him my .22 caliber repeater.

On my way to school during the first hard snowfall, it was dark and snowing pretty hard up on the ridge. The snow falling clumped up to the size of dollar bills! When I flashed on my high-beam lights it felt like I was in the Star Wars movie and just shifted into light speed! It looked pretty dang cool. In contrast, one morning when it was snowing, I actually saw the tiny individual snowflakes on my green Patagonia coat. I was so surprised! They were in all different shapes. It sure is true that they were each unique. I had to go slow since the snowplows hadn't yet plowed that far up the ridge and the car was sliding a bit. I did get snow tires. They were studded which worked great. I did have the studs removed before I drove back to Texas. They barely made it as they weren't made for hot weather. It felt weird going to school in the dark. The sun would come up around 11:00 A.M. and go back in between 3:30 and 4:00 P.M. When the sun was up, it just went across the horizon, low in the sky.

    Living out in the country I got to see some cool stuff. Like a big mother moose and it's calf wondering through my yard! Another time a single young moose came over and was looking at my car. It stood way taller than my Subaru Forester. It lay down under a spruce by the side of my house then took off a little later. Another time as I was pulling up in our driveway, I saw a flock of wild turkeys in the back yard in the snow. I had the dogs with me and was ready to get out of the car, since they had already seen the turkeys. I called Gaye to get the video camera out and start filming the turkeys before I got out of the car. After a bit, I got out and had the dogs by the leash and then they got loose and took off for the turkeys! The dogs started barking at the turkeys as they were running towards them. The turkeys flew up into the trees nearby. They all got away. You could see it in the video, the turkeys moving quickly, then running and finally flying up into the treetops. It looked so cool.

    When it snowed, I would clear the driveway, along with Coach Fraley, and made a very tall snow berm on both sides of the car that were a few feet higher than the car, leaving a trail to the stairs of the house. I also carved out a trail path for the dogs to run around in and do their business. I would shovel it to the edge of the yard. I had dug out some deep trails because of the snow. I couldn't even open the door to the storage underneath because there was now ice. I would have to pick up all the refuse the dogs left behind after all the snow had melted in May. I filled about three large trash bags full! I hadn't had any weed since we drove up here when I was driving through Oklahoma. I only had three with me for the entire trip. I didn't want to jeopardize anything. Gaye was uneasy with me even having those three. It was already October and I have been in cold turkey as far as weed goes. Gaye was able to get a little bit from someone at her work, and it was good. I also didn't have any television. Where I lived, there was no cable and I had to buy, mount and connect an outdoor antenna. The winds were picking up and the weather reports said that the wind would get as high as 70 mph. The kids were saying, "We're going to have a hurricane!" The weather was supposed to drop to minus 40 below zero. I wanted to get that antenna mounted. I climbed on a ladder on the side of the house and mounted the antenna up high on the side. The wind was picking up and I had to take off my glove to hold the screw properly. For those few seconds, Oh my! I could barely feel my hands! Finally, I got it set up so that I could watch a little TV. Although it was the coldest weather that I've ever experienced, I never got that chill that goes right to the bone, making me go into uncontrollable convulsions literally making my teeth chatter in 50 degree weather like back in Texas! I asked my students hey do you all have to leave the water faucets dripping when it freezes here? They looked at me like I'm crazy! I said, What? In, Texas, we have to let the water drip if it's going to be freezing for an extended period of time. They told me that the pipes here are six feet deep and not six inches deep! Ok, then, gotcha!

At one of our first football practices, I saw something flying and as soon as I could tell it was a bald eagle, I blew my whistle. I yelled, time! and pointed up with my finger at the eagle. The players said what? I said, look! Check it out! Again, they said, what? I said, look it's a bald eagle. They all yelled, it's just an eagle! I yelled, yeah it's an eagle! I was so excited to see one. After that, I began to notice them everywhere. There was one that would hang around a spruce tree by my house. I had to keep an eye out on my cats. Eagles are known to swoop down on them up for dinner.

At our first home football game I get there early to the field house and stadium. I ask one of the coaches, "Hey, where's the band? He says, what are you talking about? I say, the band, football game?" He didn't get it. I said, "Is the band not going to play? He said, no. They play at basketball games. Whaaat? Really? Yes, Sir. Ok, then. In Alaska, football is in its infancy compared to Texas. Maybe, that's not the right word. Let's just say, they see it a little differently here in Alaska. They introduced the players, then the coaches. I was hoping that they wouldn't say that I was from Texas. Nobody cares! And sure enough, they do say that I'm from Texas and I can hear someone yell, so what! Oh, the band did play at our last home game. They came in their street clothes. They didn't even have a band uniform. Ok, then.

One of my players was a foreign exchange student from Mexico City. He had already graduated, but wanted to stay in school one more year to learn English better. He was eighteen already and had never ever played football, but wanted to try it. He played on the Junior Varsity squad. I remember when we were playing a game in Soldotna. Diego was going to be getting the ball and run off tackle. I yelled out, ¡Te va a dar el fútbol! Siguéle al número treinta y tres! I said, you're going to get the ball! Follow number thirty-three. No one else understood, but he did. He got the ball and crossed the goal line and the referee signaled touchdown with his upright arms! Then, another referee came and said, no, he didn't score. We said, he sure did, otherwise why did the referee signal that he did. They didn't let us keep the touchdown. I tell you, I've seen some pretty terrible calls coaching, even in Texas!

Two of our games would be overnight stays, in Palmer and in Houston. They are about nine hours or so away and we would spend the night in the gym and play the next day. In Anchorage, we stopped at Dimond Center, a very nice mall. We spent some time there and went on to Palmer on one trip, then to Houston, on another. On our trip back to Homer, we were driving along the Turnagain Arm and all of a sudden, I see a school of beluga whales hugging the shoreline. I said, Hey! Check it out! Then a kid says, yeah! Nowhere but Alaska! For sure!

I thought that everything was cool between all of the coaches but, towards the end of the season there was some noticeable tension between Sam and Coach Bailey. I'm not sure what was going on, but one time in the middle of a game, I thought that they were going to duke it out right there on our sideline. Oh, hell no! Not on my watch! I had to tell them to quit acting like a couple of bitches and grow the "f" up! They calmed down a bit. Coach Daryl had to give them a talking to. I'm glad that the season was just about over. It was weird since I got along with both of them. I liked them both. Sam would go on to be the head coach. I would see him again in nine years. I would see him again when on vacation in 2008. I got to show Lydia around and we were lucky that there was a game. The bleachers face the opposing team's sideline with a beautiful view of the mountains in the background. Nicest view ever! At practice one afternoon, the kids were all by the field house. I thought, *what the hell are they waiting for?* There was a female moose and her calf at the end of the field. I said, Hey, we're burning daylight! I walk out a little way, and yelled and made a growling yell while raising my arms at the same time. The moose looked at me and wasn't impressed. Then, a player came and got me by the arm and said, "C'mon coach it'll leave in a minute." Moose kill people every year. They get stomped to death. Coach Bailey said if you're ever confronted by one, hug a tree and don't let go.

In the school building they had two wings that were two levels. In one wing you have the freshman downstairs and the sophomores upstairs. In the other wing you have the juniors downstairs and seniors upstairs. They would decorate their individual hallways for Christmas. I was in the freshmen hall and put reindeer bodies and legs with the upper half appearing that it was in stuck in the ceiling.

On one of our early fire drills, we all evacuated the building. **Confession:** It started to snow and I tell my class to start making snow balls to throw at the French class. They all looked at me and said, no, we can't do that. It's against the rules. I said, I'll play stupid and take the responsibility. Okay, then. They agreed. I said, ¡Uno, dos, tres, ¡Ataquen! We start to bombard the French class and all of the other students just look at us. After the drill, Rick came to me and said, we don't allow snowball fights here on campus. Ok, then. Sorry, I didn't know. Hehe!

Like I said earlier, Diego was from Mexico City and already eighteen. We had a good rapport and often spoke Spanish to each other. It was very nice to be able to have a conversation in Spanish. **Confession:** He approached me and asked if I could buy some cigarettes for him. He said it was hard to get them. It was way easier to score some weed than cigarettes. I think you had to be twenty-one years old to buy them. I did get him a couple of packs a couple of times. I didn't feel guilty as he was already eighteen. Another senior was this girl who came out for football. She was a pretty girl, but she was pretty tough, tougher than some boys. Her name was Bella. She was also a nationally ranked wrestling champion. She wanted to play football and so Coach Phillips let her play on the C-Team. At practice she hit this one kid when she stuck her face guard into a boy's chest. She hit him hard enough to make him cry! What? No shit. She made him cry and there's no crying in football. I mean, some of these players were huge, but rather wimpy.

One Sunday morning I wanted to go to McDonald's in town to get a new breakfast sandwich that they were advertising. So, I go and get one and on my way home, there's a curve in the road and I hit some black ice and the car spins around. It spins around and hits the snow berm on the side of the road. As I get my bearings down, I notice that there's a car coming down the road in my direction. It stops and the woman asks if I needed a ride to call someone. I said, Sure, thanks. She drove me to the Fritz Creek store and post office just down the road. I called Ben, one of the other coaches and he picked me up and took me to my car and was able to pull me out with his pick-up truck. I had to have the entire side of the Subaru replaced. Thank goodness for insurance!

Ben had borrowed a snow machine from someone and called me to see if Gaye and I would like to go. It was down the road from where we lived, a bog nearby was the perfect place to go. He picked us up and off we went. He parked the truck near a small snow bank that made it easier to unload the snow machine from his truck. He turns on the machine takes us one at a time out to the bog. Once there, we all take our turn going in quarter-mile to half-mile circles. On my turn I was able to get it up to 70 MPH! I was freaking hauling ass! I could barely see the speedometer and I didn't want to go any faster. I could see myself flying off at that speed. Instead, I slowed down and went into some unchartered territory and got the snow machine stuck in waist-high snow! Fuck! I tried and tried to get it out but couldn't. I started walking back to get Ben's and Gaye's attention. It was hard after walking in that high snow! Finally, I made it to our track and it was easier. They followed me back and we got the machine out. We were all so tired after that hike. It was probably close to two miles to get them and two miles back to the machine. He took us one at-a-time back to the truck. That was really fun!

As far as coaching football, I didn't even know how much stipend I was going to get. Barry, the Athletic Director had called a meeting to let us know how much our checks would be. I was quite disappointed to learn that it would only be $1000! That's practically nada! In Texas I would later get seven times that! I still enjoyed it as I got to see some of the state. I would coach baseball for free!

Some of my students told me that they regularly get their snow machines up to 120 MPH! I thought, *No freaking way!* That is, until they showed me a video of themselves! I could not believe it. They would ride up on the mountains and jump with the machine forty, fifty or more feet! I mean they caught some serious air. It was hard to believe.

I used to rollerblade down the hallways and around campus during my conference period. I was amusing to some of the staff. I always made it a point to say hi or go by and visit with the secretaries like Kamy and Rikki! They are often the ones who know what's going

A CHICANO SPANISH TEACHER

on. I would bring my video camera and record some of the different classes. I would walk in and just start recording. The science room was the best, as far as having cool stuff to video. He had a stuff polar bear in one corner and a Rasta moose skeleton set up as well. It was a moose skeleton with a dread-lock wig. He also had huge King Crabs, the red one and a blue one. Gaye and I also befriended Lizzy, the custodian. She was such a sweetheart. She was an elderly Japanese-American and short of stature. Her husband was an artist and she gave me a beautiful print of one of his paintings of a landscape with the Russian Orthodox Church with the mountains and volcano in the background.

At night when driving out on the highways you have to keep your eyes open looking for moose. I was driving and Gaye yelled out for me to stop. I immediately stopped about a foot from a moose. It would have been bad if I had hit it. Often times, they get clipped in the knees by the car and fall towards the windshield, which is what would have happened. Whew!

I had one student bring in a huge walrus tusk that her father had found on some beach on the North Slope. I think it's where he worked at the time. It was large, heavy and thick. You could probably hurt someone pretty bad with it. It was solid ivory, dang I had never seen anything like it. I was always seeing new and exciting things! A good thing about being a teacher is that we can get our cars worked on if the school has an Auto Tech department, like getting the oil changed. They do other small stuff as well. I took in the Forester for an oil change. The students, a couple of football players were going to do the job. They happened to mistakenly remove the plug to the transmission fluid pan rather than the oil pan. Then, they added more oil to the already full oil pan. The teacher calls me to let me know that it's going to be a little longer than expected. They had to drain the oil, change the filter, add oil, and finally add transmission fluid. When I went to get the car one of the kids, the Varsity running back told me, hey Coach, I like your music. I think I had Ultraspank or Spineshank in the tape deck.

I used to take the dogs out for a walk across East End Road to a thicket of small tree at the edge of McNeil Canyon. It was a little spooky at times when I thought that there could be a bear. About almost a mile down the road, just past McNeil Elementary is where the pavement ends. This is literally the end of the westernmost road in North America connected to the highway system. Well, it used to end there. There was a big garbage dumpster where people would take their garbage. I would go every couple of weeks or so. There was a big tree by the dumpster that had big claw marks a bear had made at some time, so I knew they were out there. I had to be careful crossing the road. Sometimes cars would haul freaking ass down the highway. I mentioned this to the students and they all said, yeah, those are Russians. They crash their cars and the government buys them a new one. They didn't say why, but shit, what a deal!

The girl that played football I mentioned earlier, Bella, had me lay down on some fresh snow that was falling during lunch and showed me how to make a snow angel. She now appears every so often on the show, *Alaska: The Last Frontier* as one of Eve's friends and neighbors. They actually live down the road from where I used to live. When I visited Homer in 2008, they had paved the road further down for miles and miles. I had to turn around and head back. I don't know if the road goes down all the way to where the Kilcher's live, the family in the show.

You know being a teacher you're really not supposed to give kids a ride. Just to keep anything from happening. Well, Gaye and I were driving home and I saw one of my football players walking home. He was going down East End Road. I knew he lived near where I did, so I stopped and offered him a ride. I turned right onto a dirt road and continued down the ridge to his house. Shit, it was pretty far off of the road. He would have walked around twelve miles or so to get to his house. I think someone would have given him a ride. People are nice like that here.

In my Spanish 3 class, we translated some letters that the elementary kids wrote to some pen pals in Peru. The letters were in

A CHICANO SPANISH TEACHER

English, and my class translated them to Spanish. In one of the letters one of the students writes, we make snow forts and have snow ball fights. Well, I wanted to know what snow forts were. On one very cold day I took my class outside. There was about three and a half feet of snow on the ground. The snow came up to my thighs. It was so freaking hard to walk through it when making a trail. We went to a spot where there were some trees and quite a bit of deep snow. We divided ourselves into two teams. We started to make a wall or snow fort where you could take cover from the snow balls. Oh! Now I know. Let's get it on! We proceeded to have an awesome snow ball fight. We all had so much fun! After about an hour we were all so freaking cold. In the classroom I had some hot chocolate waiting for us! It was so, so good! The kids couldn't believe that we just had an awesome snow ball fight here at school! I had parking lot duty one week after school. I would climb up a snow berm piled in the middle parking lot where I would watch and direct traffic from. I did this a couple of times in February. Teacher's duty has never been like this. Another new experience for sure.

In the Kenai Peninsula Borough School District, all the teachers were given a $250 stipend called a discretionary check. We could use it in any way we saw fit. We could pay bills or whatever. I thought, this would be good to have a big class party. So that's what I did. This was near the end of the school year. We had gone to Bishop's Beach where there were picnic tables and barbeque pits so that we could grill some fajitas. I was able to bring out a couple of classes out there. Some of the kids helped cook the meat and it was a great time. What a view!

I was upstairs in the library on the outside deck. Little pellets of snow start to fall. They are like tiny snowballs where you could crush it between your fingers easily, not ice. One of the kids says after I ask, what's this? He says, hail. I said, this isn't hail. He says yes it is. I told him that hail is hard like ice and they can be anywhere from quarter-sized to golf ball-sized to softball-sized balls of ice, at least in Texas. Also the rain is different. Not the huge-ass rain drops like in Texas that can give you a concussion. Ok, so I'm exaggerating. But like where I lived on the ridge. The rain cloud would come up from the bay like a mist and begin to climb up the ridge to my house and over it to the top of the hill. I never saw a rain drop.

    Coach Daryl lived off of the main road coming into Homer. He had a very nice home. He showed me a picture with a big pipe lying in the snow. I asked, what's that? He said the top of my kids swing set. Last winter they had a huge snowfall. Anyway, we had an ice cream social with the football players and the coaches and their wives. It's customary to remove your shoes before entering a home. I took a picture of all the kids' shoes in the mud room. One weekend, we had a little get together there. Just passed his yard there was a slope downhill where we could snowboard and or sled down. We were up pretty high with a clear view of Mount Augustine. It was a volcano, one that looked stereotypical with a cone-shape. The following year I was invited to go on a hunting trip there on the island where the volcano is. We would get flown in, stay there for three days, and get picked up. It wouldn't come to fruition though. There was a snow berm at the bottom of the slope, blocking passage off of the cliff. As I was hauling ass down the slope towards the berm, I suddenly realized that it would be solid ice and not soft snow, so I braced myself for a good thump. I hit it hard. Before I hit it, I tried to slow myself down with my hands. Coach Baley came down with his snow machine to take me back up to the top of the hill. On the way up, he was pulling me while I was laying frontwards on the sled. The road back was quite rough. I bounced hard on the ice as he dragged up while I was on the sled. A couple of days later I had to go to the hospital because it hurt to breathe. The physician's assistant who was attending me was a parent of one of my students. She asked me if I had a problem with her seeing me. I said, no, of course not. What's the matter with me? They took X-rays. It seemed that I had bruised ribs. Thank goodness that was all it was. They were quite sore for a few days.

    So, in my Spanish 3 class that translated the letters from the elementary kids got invited to the elementary school for a party. We all went and they had so much food. As we were walking towards the school, I noticed that the kids on the hill that was covered in snow were all carrying some kind of blue rolls. I asked one of the kids, what that was they were carrying? He tells me that they are roll-up sleds. I said, let me see. I ask to borrow one and get on it. I get one of my students to give me a little push. I then went down the hill hauling butt! It was so much fun! I had to buy my own little plastic sled. I went to the stadium where there was a driveway on the side that slanted downward. I would get on the sled and take each of my dogs down for a little ride. They reluctantly stayed on with me. They were such good sports. I miss them.

In the winter after having snowed some, I decided to shovel the roof. It was flat and had a metal covering on it. There was already at least three feet on the roof. I mainly used my scooper shovel and push the snow over the edge of the roof onto the wooden walkway in the front of the house. It was dark and sort of eerie, the sky that is. I wanted to hurry so that I wouldn't be caught outside in a storm. Well, the ladder fell onto the deck and Gaye was not around. I decided that I would jump into the pile of snow on the wooden walkway. I went straight through and landed on the platform hard.

Sometimes at night, I would let my dogs out to do their business. At 3:00 A.M. early one morning I was going to let them back inside. When I went to call them, they were both looking up at the night sky. The aurora was visible and quite active. It looked so cool. I felt so lucky to be there and to see it. I told Ben about it the next day and he told me to call him next time I see it. I saw it several more times and I did call and wake his ass up. Another time after I had let the dogs out, they began barking and barking. I went out quickly only to find that they had gotten into it with a porcupine! Shit! I finally got them into the house. They both had quills all over their snouts. What the hell did they think was going to happen? I got them inside and gave them a tranquilizer to try and calm them down a bit. They both settled down some, but it was going to be a long night. We tried to make them as comfortable as possible, this was not easy. We called the vet and he said to come in the morning. It couldn't get here fast enough! They woke up with some pain, but at last, we dropped them off on the way to school and picked them up after school. The vet had to do surgery to get the quills out. Other people told me that it's happened several times with their dog. They don't learn!

That Thanksgiving, we made the drive to Anchorage to spend it with my cousin Sonny and his family. It was cold and there was quite a bit of snow on the ground already. Passing through Soldotna the bank temperature gauge said 1 degree! The drive takes about four hours. The kids were always talking about going to Anchorage for a day and driving back like it was no big deal. I guess to them, since everything is so far apart, it doesn't seem like that far. For me, it was like driving from Alice, TX to Houston, a long frigging drive! Only in an emergency would I do that as a round-trip. Well, we get to Anchorage and the dogs are outside on the back porch. It's about seventeen degrees and they're shivering. I asked my cousin Sonny if I could keep them in the garage which he gladly allowed. The garage has a heater that he turned on for them. They were so good, they didn't even bark once! We spent the night and visited with him, his wife and two girls. They were so cute! We headed on back. The drive is beautiful! The mountains along the Turnagain Arm had all these long iced over waterfalls. It looked so cool. In the summer it turns to liquid.

Ben had gone hunting and had some moose meat. He gave me a couple of very thick steaks. Dang, they were so good, tender and very tasty. The best meat that I've ever had to that point in my life! Oh I was excited to have gotten invited to go on a moose hunt for the following year.

During the Christmas Break, we took a drive to the Spit. I had heard from the kids that there are all of these eagles congregating, waiting for the "Fish Lady." We get there and there is a short line of cars waiting to drive by. There are signs telling the motorists not to get out of their cars. I never saw anyone out of them either. What a sight, hundreds and hundreds of Bald Eagles and some Golden Eagles too! There were adults and some juveniles, but they all were very big.

A CHICANO SPANISH TEACHER

Even the Ravens were there although not in the abundance as the eagles. We took some video and added it to a video we made for our families. It was incredible. **Sidebar:** It's illegal for anyone to own an eagle feather, unless you are a Native American. Most all of the kids there had one. I got offered one, but I politely refused, although I AM 33% Native American!

I had two student aides. One of them was gone for about a week on a fishing trip with her parents. She brought me back an f-load of ling cod! It was so good! I was very appreciative and she was happy to give me some. My other aide was also a very nice girl. One of the coolest prom stories, her prom date came to pick her up in a helicopter and took her flight-seeing! How cool was that! I did see her about nine years later at the Anchorage Airport when Lydia and I came for a visit. As I was arriving, she was leaving and I saw her from a distance and yelled her name out. She came over with her younger sister. Her sister was so pretty, they both were. We said our hello's and went about our way. It was so nice to see her, small world.

There at the High School in Homer, the kids take off on vacation all throughout the year. One of my students was gone for two weeks to the Cook Islands. He had gotten a tattoo on his shoulder done the old school Pacific Island kind of way with a piece of bamboo. It was of some fertility god. He was also one of the baseball players. Another two of my students, who were also sisters in levels 1 and 2, had gone to Iquitos, Peru. They brought me back a beaded necklace with a piranha lower jaw. It looked so cool! **Sidebar:** The piranha necklace, along with my P.A.D.I Divemaster Certificate, my Texas-Shaped Plaque for Teacher of the Year in Wimberley, and my Beatles picture of them playing on the rooftop of Abbey Road Studios were all in a box that I left in my portable classroom before the summer was out. When we got moved to the new building at Hays, the box got misplaced! Shit, I was pissed! I loved that Beatle picture! It's always nice to receive little gifts from students. I wouldn't accept anything of real value, souvenirs are ok. They were also there for two weeks. The schools allow this, or didn't mind because in the summer many of the students work in the fishing industry. Shit, some make up to 40K and more! Some teachers just teach as a side gig when they're not fishing. I heard one story where this boat took off with a net to gather the catch and brought it around to the main ship and brought in a catch work about 180K!

In my Spanish 2 classes when I am teaching commands, I like to have the students teach the class how to do something. I have them use at least ten different commands. It can't be a two-step skill either. One year a student did a presentation, "How to Change a Flat Tire." I didn't know how to say "jack" in Spanish and found out its "gato." Yes, like cat. Anyway, these two students asked me if they could do a combo lesson on "How to Halibut Fish." Sure, I said, and then one of the kids asked if I wanted to come with them fishing. Hell yeah! I said. One of the kid's parents had a crab-fishing boat. We met at the Homer harbor where the boat was. It was big. While leaving the harbor, I thought I was seeing a bear in the water! I asked the kids, what's that? Oh, that's a seal. It was very big. As we're heading out, the dad offers me some coffee. It's horrible and doesn't settle too well. We're out at sea and the next I know, I have to hurl. I go over to the edge of the boat and start throwing up. I get over it quickly and have a laugh. No one makes fun because they know that very easily it could be them. The kids are great and do everything for me, bait and gaff the halibut into the boat.

About mid-day we went across Kachemak Bay over to Seldovia to grab a bite to eat. We pulled into the bay and parked by the pier. We had to climb up about twenty feet or so to get to the top of the pier. That's how high the tide gets. Right then, it was at low tide and it gets all the way to the top of the pier. We walked into town and there was only one four-way stop sign. We went into a quaint little restaurant and got some burgers for lunch. It was very small and not much to see. It was interesting to see the other side of the bay. We head on back and finish getting our catch. We're allowed only two halibut per day so we end up tossing back the smaller ones. It can get very tiring in a hurry. We get back to the harbor at dusk and we're there about another two hours. The guys are filleting the halibut. They give me a trash bag full. I kept it in my freezer for a short while. Adam, the French teacher offered to smoke it for me. I gladly thanked him. Everyone up here has a smoker and luckily got to enjoy it! Adam had called me up early one evening. He said the tide was going to be very low in the bay where you could walk way out and get some mussels. I said, sure! I met him at the Spit and we had our rubber boots and he had some special tools to harvest the mussels. I believe they were blue mussels. Indeed, the water had receded a good bit. After some time, the tide started to come in. Adam said, okay, we need to hurry and we beat the tide just in time! We also took home some mussels! I enjoyed all of the experiences that I've had here in Alaska. Life is good and I'm so lucky!

The Art teacher, Don Bart invited me to go fly fishing. Again, we met at the Spit, at the Fishing Hole. It was a small inlet where the water would rush in and out through a break in the land. We were there at the mouth of the Fishing Hole hoping to catch a big King. It took a little getting used to, but once I got the hang of it, it was so much fun. We didn't catch anything. It was still fun just being out there! He had a pic of himself when he was a bit younger when he had a long Mohawk and was flying through the air upside down doing tricks on skis! Pretty cool pic. He wrote in my book, hook 'em, gaff 'em, sleep on ice! Let's catch some next time!

It was in the spring when Daryl, Ben, and I went to a Coach of the Year Conference in Portland, Oregon. It was for three-nights and the first night we went to the Cabaret Club. It was a total nudity strip club. Daryl didn't want to go, I think he felt guilty. I just wanted to grab a bite to eat with some sights and maybe help out a working girl. I say that in a nice way. I mean who are we to judge. I like to pick one girl and give her most of my money. There at the club was this Alicia Silverstone look-alike. She was at my side for a few hours until, of course, I ran out of money. Once my money is gone, that's it no more. There was also this other dancer who was a splitting image of one of my mixed Native American students. Wow! I couldn't believe it. When I got back to Homer, I asked that one student, you weren't in Portland this past weekend were you? She looked at me and said, No!

Homer didn't have a baseball team. Ben wanted to start one. He bought all of the uniforms on his credit card and set up games. We had two other parents that helped out as coaches. I made the line-up and batting order. We had a decent team and a better record than the football team. We traveled to Palmer for a multi-day tournament. It was quite enjoyable. I got to see more of the state while coaching football and baseball. The coach from Kodiak Island sent us plane tickets so that we could go and play baseball. On the short flight of about an hour and a half, I experienced the worst air turbulence that I ever have! I mean the plane shook hard. It would just drop all of a sudden, and then steady itself. The view was spectacular of the mountain chain of the Alaska Peninsula. Once there we stayed the night in the boy's dressing room which was a bit more comfortable and warm than the gym. It was a long night and it poured rain. In the morning it continued pouring hard. This is the only place I heard it rain hard like this in Alaska. I didn't see it, but could only hear it. I asked their coach if we were going to be able to play. He told me, we'll be alright coach. I said Ok. When we get to the field it is a black gravel infield with no grass. They got a steamroller and flattened it out right before the game. Play ball! The infield was fine, but there was standing water in the outfield. The temperature was in the 30's, but with the windchill it felt like 17 degrees! I had to do the book. To begin with, I don't do a very nice and neat book. I've never been good at it. I could barely feel my fingers! It was so cold that I had to climb inside a truck cab to stay out of the wind. You should have seen the book! Oh my, how terrible! It looked like a bunch of chicken scratch!

It's already May and I tell Rick that I'm resigning my position. I wasn't sure if I was going to have a job. Some positions had gotten cut and were given pink slips as they called them. Foreign language was an elective and not a core subject like Math and Science. Therefore, I wasn't sure if Spanish would get cut next. Gaye was homesick and wanted to return. I remember when I saw my first bald eagle on the

A CHICANO SPANISH TEACHER

football practice field; I thought that this was the place that I would retire. How would that have been, but reality sets in and I agree that we would move back to Texas. We made arrangements to rent another U-Haul truck. It was half as much only $1500. It seemed like we were there for just a short while, which we were. I would leave without having a secure job to go to and would have to pound the pavement to find one. The plan was to move in with Gaye's parents while we would look for jobs and a place to live. I left the day of a baseball game. I stopped to say my goodbyes to everyone and headed off. On the way out we stopped at the Eagle Grocery Store and picked up a few items for the road. The last student that I saw was a football player who I would see next time on the show *Deadliest Catch*. He would be a hand on the Ramblin Rose crab ship. **Sidebar:** We all got conned by Coach Ben! He was a con man. He didn't have a teaching degree or anything like he said he had. No wonder I always made the line-ups and made sure the other coaches were well-informed. What happened was, Gaye had gotten a call by a friend of Ben's wife. Apparently, she had called the police on Ben for domestic spousal abuse because allegedly he had shoved her. I can't say for sure, but the police came to the baseball field to arrest him. He asked the cops not to do it in front of the players. They respected his wish and escorted him to their car. Gaye was left to call Ben's parents wherever they lived. They answered the phone asking, what has he done now? He had us all fooled. He was such a nice guy though.

We drove through Anchorage and made it all the way to Tok where we spent the night. The truck was on Empty for the last 250 miles until it move just passed and we arrived in Tok! Thank you Lord! We left early in the morning. We stopped at the last store/outpost before going into the Yukon Territory. We drove all the way to Whitehorse and spent the night. The following day traveling through the Yukon just as we crossed the Yukon River just passed the bridge, there was an incline and all of a sudden, the U-Haul trucks stops. I pull off as far as I can. I get out and put some safety reflector triangles to set out to warn other vehicles coming up the road toward us. Gaye drives ahead to the next town, I think it was Watson Lake, where they have all these different signs from all over the place. Anyway she calls the telephone number that I have in case of emergencies. They direct her to a garage and they arrange to come and pick up the truck and get it going again. We pull into a small place called Beaver Post. It's not as far as Watson Lake and can just go there in the morning. This place had like little houses with a bed and bathroom. They were comfortable and cozy. They also had a very cool country store outpost. It had all kinds of interesting things. They were several wolf pelts of all sorts, very expensive, just a lot of cool stuff. The following morning we all get into the Subaru and head on to Watson Lake to pick up the truck. We continue on our way and when going by Muncho Lake, the water was such a deep blue, it was so beautiful. I wished that we would have been able to check it out for a little stay, but we were on a mission to get back.

It took us eleven days to get to Alaska and only nine to return to Texas. When we were in British Colombia, we were going through Laird, where the hot springs are. We had lunch at a nearby restaurant. Just by the side of the road was a buffalo just lying there. I wanted to get a closer look, but didn't want disturb it or worse, get attacked. After lunch, we decide to go to the hot springs. We pull into the parking lot. We crack the windows for the animals and the weather is cool anyway, they wouldn't get hot and we wouldn't be too long. We go and check in and get a locker and get into our bathing suits. There are wooden walkways through the forest to get to the springs. It's really beautiful, but we were on the lookout for bears. They like the springs too. They had warning signs saying to give them the right of way. I can't believe some people need signs. It's a freaking bear! The pools have different temperatures. It felt so good! I can understand why bears like it too.

Coming back into the lower 48, we stopped at St. Mary's in Montana and I had a buffalo steak that I thought was the best cut of meat that I ever had. It was so good and delicious. Just down a little way was the Sun Road. It's the road in the Forrest Gump movie where he's running in a valley surrounded by mountains. I really wanted to go, but decided that it wouldn't be a good idea to leave the U-Haul truck there sitting in a parking lot for any amount of time. Driving further into Montana, I finally see a bear by the side of the road. I tell Gaye with the walkie-talkie that I was going to stop to get some footage. I quickly pulled over and got my video camera. I started filming. It was a small black bear and was running. It was putting as much ground between us as possible. I wished that I would have been able to video the mother brown bear and cub that I had seen a few days earlier driving by Lake Kluane.

A little further down into Montana, we stopped at the Little Bighorn Battlefield near Garry Owen. We walked out there only a little as there were warning signs for rattlesnakes. It was an area of grassy hills. They also had an excellent gift shop. I got what was my favorite t-shirt, at the time, of a Blackfoot Warrior. It looked so cool. I also had to have a Sitting Bull poster. The only one they had was on display up high on a wall. They took it down for me and sold it. It took me a while to get it framed. I also got a few Native American post cards that I kept. We also went into a Blackfoot Reservation gift shop. They had so many things, all kinds of crafts, really cool stuff. We couldn't spend as much time as we would have liked since we had the cats and dogs waiting in car for us every time we stopped and got out.

We finally made it to New Braunfels. We stopped near the Oklahoma-Texas border to visit with Gaye's aunt and uncle. It was June and very hot. Shit, I already missed Alaska! I had to find a job and finally found one at Hays High School in the Kyle-Buda area, yea!

8. Full Circle

I had returned to Hays High School. It's where I started my teaching career with my student teaching. As a matter of fact, Mrs. Claire was retiring and I think another teacher also retired. They needed someone who could teach Advance Placement level for Spanish. I got hired to teach that and the other upper-level Spanish 3 classes. In my interview for the job, I told them that I had baseball experience; they needed an assistant coach for softball. I agreed to do it, to get my foot in the door and get hired. It worked. I had to go to the new teacher orientation. There's always so much freaking information that they give you. It's insane and we have to learn it and know it. Every school has its own type of protocol and procedures. They use different computer software say for, attendance. I liked that they used First Class. It was easy and convenient to use.

When I interviewed with the principal for the teaching position, he had asked me if it was important to me if the students liked me. I looked at him, and said, of course! If they like me they'll want to come to my class, which is what I want. He told me that I had answered correctly, or like he had wanted me to answer. He said that he's had many teachers answer differently that never got hired. The department chair was Mrs. French. She enjoyed what power she thought she had as a department chair. It was a real trip working under her. I just tried to be respectful.

It had been a long summer, staying at my in-laws. They were very nice people. I stayed mostly in our room watching television and playing with the dogs and cats. When school started, I was commuting to school from New Braunfels. At the end of September,

Gaye asks me for a divorce and I move out the next day. I went to stay with Adrian and Rose for a month in their home in Austin. I would take leftovers for lunch the following day. I lucked out as Rose was a good cook! That month I would drive every weekend and pick up the dogs, Alex and Max and would take them for a drive! I missed them so much and also the cats, although I didn't take them for a drive as well. I would see them through the fence. I did that for the month I was living in Austin.

    I drove to work from Austin now. In my spare time I looked for a place and found a new double-wide trailer with a lot in the Quail Ridge neighborhood of Kyle. It was on the outskirts of town, near Interstate 35. It would be a while before I would be able to move in. All that was left to connect was the electricity and water. I asked if I could still move in and they said yes, but that I wouldn't have electricity and water for a week. No problem. I just wanted to get my dogs and cats. I told my soon-to-be ex-wife that I would keep them all. We lived in our new house for that first week without power and water. The housing company had given me a couple of cases of water and a case of the Duraflame fire logs. I only had a small sleeper loveseat where we would all lay on in front of the fireplace, me, the two dogs and three cats. I was happy once again. If I had to pee I would just go out to the backyard. There was a rest area by the entrance of our subdivision on I35. I could also go there if I had to. I would shower at school in the Coach's office locker room before school each day, then head on to class.

    I was a roaming teacher and didn't really have my own classroom. I had to have a file cabinet in a couple of places to keep all of my files and papers. I had plenty. I didn't like that any student could sign up for an AP class without having any type of stipulation, say capability or teacher recommendation. I had plenty of students who just wanted the AP label on their record of classes taken for their transcripts without being capable of doing the work and passing. Back then, the AP Spanish Language Exam was way more difficult than it is nowadays. Today, they don't even include a grammar section.

In that AP class I did have a student I'll call Jacque. He was very smart and a cool kid. He got sent to the Alternative Discipline Center because he had gone to a basketball game and his eyes were red, allegedly. He was confronted by the security cop at the game. He was from the Hays Sheriff's department and as redneck as they come. Jacque told the officer that yes, he was indeed stoned. He actually told the truth and they took him away. He didn't even have any on him and they still acted as if he did. He told me that his other teachers sort of shunned him. He was a cool kid and I reassured his parents, who by the way, were so nice, that I would do whatever I could to help him out. I'm sure they appreciated that. While he was at the center, all of the kids there called him, The Professor. He was so smart! We actually became friends and he invited me to his wedding. It was out in the country and was so cool. When he graduated, since he was in the top ten percent of his class, he got to choose his favorite teacher. I was so surprised. I was called in to take a picture with him for a book. The Hays Education Foundation gave the students and the favorite teachers a dinner banquet at the University of Texas campus in Austin. I could have invited a guest, but didn't have one, so his parents asked if they could bring their daughter, no problem. I haven't heard from him in a while. He was working as a physicist in Houston, last I heard. I've been so lucky to meet such awesome people. Under our photo he wrote something that I heard somewhere, but in order to be happy you need to do three things, 1. Be able to love, 2. Have courage, and 3. Have a good sense of humor. He included that but in a more poetic way!

When the New Year passed, it was time to start my softball coaching experience. I showed up to the first practice. They were already on the field since they had seventh period athletics and I was in the classroom all day until after school. So I walk up to where the head coach is just stand there and watch the girls catch and throw going through some in-field drills. Oh snap! I couldn't believe how good they were! I mean, they didn't even throw like girls! They threw like guys not girls. Oh, they were indeed good. A couple of them came

A CHICANO SPANISH TEACHER

up to me and told me that they played Select; I didn't know what that meant at the time. I asked them if they could, catch, throw, run and hit. They just walked away. Anyone can say anything. Let's see some action! I remember speaking to a parent. He wanted his daughter to get more playing time, and she did until the basketball girls came out. She couldn't produce. Some of the parents were pretty intense. We did have two undefeated seasons in district while I was an assistant. We had an ace pitcher who ended up going and playing in college along with another player or two from those teams.

During my second year of coaching softball, we had a phenomenal catcher. She was however a bit troubled and often found herself in trouble. She had violated one of our team rules; I can't remember which one but most or all of the girls were against her starting in the game. I agreed. I like to think that I live by certain principles that I cannot or do not want to compromise. I mean, if you don't have principles, what do you have? Like most coaches that I know or have known, are only interested in one thing, winning, period. Whatever principles there might have been are no longer that important. Well, the coach did let that particular player start the game. Our team morale was low even though we had an undefeated season. I have always considered myself a teacher first, then a coach. After all, if it weren't for the teaching position, I wouldn't have a coaching position, duh!

The following year, I was the head coach of the junior varsity. Neither team played well that year, besides I really didn't want to coach softball anymore, but couldn't just quit until I found another coach to replace me. One afternoon after school, I stopped by Dairy Queen. I went in and ordered and while I was waiting, I turned around and saw Lou's parents, Louie Sr. and his mom! I was so surprised to see them and they were just as surprised. It was so good to see them. They told me that Lou was having a house built here in Kyle and they would be moving here soon. Great! It had been a while since I'd seen him. We reconnected. Another time I went to DQ to order some tacos. When I pulled up to pay, I noticed that it was a student of mine and a football player working there. He gave me my order and I asked him how much and handed him a ten dollar bill. Well, he wouldn't take it. He said, coach, your money's no good here and refused to let me pay. He wouldn't take the money. I told him that I really wanted to pay, but it was futile. I drove off and I would not go back to DQ for quite some time, not knowing if he was working or not.

I was already coaching football as a B-team coach calling the offense. I did scouting for the varsity football team. I was told by the Head Coach/Athletic director that he had heard that I knew football. Yes Sir, I said. He then asked if I could coach. Once again, yes Sir. I would soon be quite busy during the football season. In coaching football, I felt much more at ease than coaching girls. Guys were easier to coach, for some reason. I wasn't a yeller coach and I also never used profanity. I always thought that it was very unprofessional and I didn't like to hear it from other coaches either. None of the coaches that I worked with used profanity, at least not as a normal occurrence.

One surprise when I started working there at Hays High, was finding out that one of me and my father's all-time favorite wrestler, Ivan Putski, was the parking security guy there on campus. I had visited with him at a drumming ceremony while still married to my ex-wife. He had given my dad and I and autographed picture of himself. Pretty cool, my dad thought so too!

When it came time to do our scouting report, Kevin and I would go and buy a bunch of breakfast tacos at Helen's in Buda. I made sure to order some barbacoa tacos. I didn't know if any of the coaches had ever tried any. Sure enough, I don't think any of them had. Well, they were all gringos! I mean, they were in flour tortillas, not corn. I prefer them in corn, but they were still quite good. They asked, Sonny what kind of tacos are these? I said, they're good, ¿no? Just eat them! They were all happy. No one had ever brought tacos to a scouting report on Saturday morning. I would also later bring all kinds of cakes that Lydia would make for me to take to the coaches. They loved it! They couldn't wait for us to do our scouting report! I did spend a lot of time there in the coach's office cutting and editing tape. I would be able to get some technology credit which was required as part of my on-going

A CHICANO SPANISH TEACHER

professional development. I was still doing basic level stuff. **Confession:** Although I got trained and was able to do PowerPoint presentations, I never did. Not once, not twice, zero, nada for the whole thirty-some years of my career as a teacher! I always taught old-school style. I did use videos, DVDs and slides when I first started and the internet.

The morning of September 11, 2001, I was at home watching the news, and saw the breaking news as the first plane struck the World Trade Center. It was shocking to say the least. As I kept watching, a little later the next plane hits the other building. I knew then that America would never be the same. I remember when I got to school and went to practice. The kids were sort of in a daze as we adults were and I think that most of the country was in a daze and shocked about what had just happened. The people seemed united against the terrorists who attacked New York City. I wish we could unite once again against the terrorists who attacked Washington D.C. on January 6, 2021! If we don't do something to hold them accountable, they will attack again and they are planning it as we speak! Wake the fuck up America!

Lou was a big help to me. He would go to my house to let the dogs out and feed the cats. I could call on him when I knew that I was going to be late coming home from some game. One time when I got home, the back door was completely wide-open! Oh shit! I looked and everyone was still inside, both dogs and the three cats. At the time, one of Louie's daughters, Livvy was in Kindergarten at some Christian school. Her teacher wanted to see what the students would do if she fainted. So, she pretended to faint, and fell on the floor. Livvy, being the bold little girl that she was, straddled the teacher's chest and slapped the crap out of her, saying, "In the name of Jesus, Rise!" as she lifted both her open hands to the Lord. How funny! One early afternoon the sky was getting dark and there had been a tornado spotted nearby. I gave Louie a call and asked, hey man, can I come on over until the storm passes? He said yeah, and bring everybody. Cool. The dogs were so well behaved. They never barked or anything like that. The cats were fine in their crates. As soon as it passed, I head on back home, let's go everyone!

Speaking of storms, after that first year, I was given my own classroom. It would be in a portable building out in the back part of the school campus. I would turn into the first parking lot there at school and continue driving on a dirt road to the portable building. It was late in the school day and there was a storm going on. My class was still in the portable. We could hear it just pouring and the wind was howling. All of a sudden, the door flies open and one of the assistant principals, Mr. Puente yells, we're evacuating to the band hall. It was a solid building close by. While he was yelling it out at us, the rain was flying sideways and he was getting drenched. **Confession:** As the students were following him to the band hall, I went straight to my car and drove home! I had my dogs and cats to take care of. There was actually a tornado that touched down nearby. The people that went into the band hall were there until 10:00 P.M. that night! Good thing I left!

In the summer of 2002, Lou and I took a trip to Cozumel. We both were recently divorced and had just reconnected. I'd been talking about scuba diving as always and he got himself his open-water scuba certification! Freaking awesome! We went for a week and had a blast diving and just being together in Mexico. I hadn't been to Cozumel in a few years and had missed my island terribly. The diving was good. All we had was our mask, fins and snorkel and we brought them as part of our carry-on luggage. I told the flight attendant that we would be ready to evacuate in case we crashed in the ocean. She didn't think it was funny.

I had been contacted by the principal about a teacher trying to get a job there at the high school. They wanted to know if I knew who he was. It was Mr. Wayne Carr. I told them yeah! He's a good teacher, we taught together at the University in graduate school. I thought, great! He can start teaching the Advanced Placement classes since I knew he could. He taught for a short while only then took another job. I eventually had to begin teaching the AP classes once again. Oh well, what you gonna do? I took over his class in January at the beginning of the new semester. I had in my portable building classroom my two hammocks hanging! I would use them as a positive reinforcement for the students. If they had done something good or that I liked I would let them lay in it during class while we were doing our lesson.

In the spring our department would have Foreign Language Week for all of the foreign language students. We had races and games. For example, in one game, at one of the tennis court a teacher would ask a question to a row of three students who were all on different teams. After they heard the questions, they would run across the tennis court to another teacher to give them the answer. The first one who got there to tell the teacher would get a point and the team with the most would win. We also had prizes and stuff. We might also play soccer or softball. I would sometimes take my classes to play softball against Mrs. Kate's classes. It was a nice break to be able to do that.

In that AP class that I took over, I had one student, her name was Pía. She was a nice girl. All of the kids were pretty decent. At this level they are usually more mature anyway. Well, she tells me that I should meet her mother. I'm thinking, *What?? Why would I even entertain the thought?* And then, I can't believe I asked, do you have a picture? She shows me, and I think I said, ¡Oh que bonita! What was I thinking? She gave me her email address. I took it, although I still can't believe I took it. Now I hadn't dated anyone for over three years since my separation in September of 2000. It was now 2003. I remember asking her, what's your mother's zodiac sign, she answered Leo. I thought, *Oh shit, this could be trouble!* Well, I send Pía's mother, Lydia, an email. I told her that I couldn't believe that I was doing this. This was new for her too. She was divorced and living and working in Austin. She worked at the *Austin American Statesman* newspaper as an accountant. We decided to meet and I invited her to a softball game. After the Junior Varsity game, I went up to the stands where she was sitting and introduced myself. It was awkward with all the people everywhere, with eyes on us and me not paying attention to the game or even being on the field. Ah, they didn't need me anyway. So, we talk a bit and afterwards, she drove me back to the high school campus where my car was parked. We talk some more and then a security cop knocks on my window wanting to know who I was. I told him that I was a coach and he left, which was my cue to get going. I tried to kiss her but, no way José, hold your horses! So, I kissed her hand. She did let me take her to dinner. We went to get some burgers at Grin's in San Marcos, a pretty burger place since my college days. To start our conversation she pounds the table and says she's a George Bush supporter! I'm thinking, o*h fuck! Really? At the time, the worst person in the world?* I wasn't sure what to do. Should I just let this play out and see where it goes? It's what I did. Other than politics, we got along great. She soon discovered the error of her ways. I think it was just residual baggage from a previous relationship. Despite her fear of the water, she got herself scuba certified. She moved in with me after I had known her only a month. What the…? What was I thinking? Before Lydia could move in she had to be approved by Rusty, Chica, Alex and Max, my cats and dogs. They all approved quite quickly too. **Confession:** I used to leave a zip-loc bag of roaches underneath my coffee table. Lydia had warned me before that the dogs might get to them. I didn't really think they would until Alex did. He ate almost a whole bag of roaches of some good shit! Fuck! He got so wasted that he couldn't even get up to go to the bathroom outside and peed all over himself. I thought, *should I take him to the vet?* I didn't take him and he slowly started to come out of it. He mostly slept. I continued to keep a baggie of roaches under the table and once again Lydia had warned me. I said, he wouldn't do that again, well, he did! I quit putting it there. I should have known since he had already eaten a bowl of Hershey Kisses, foil and chocolate. I later scooped his poop that had different colors of foil in it! I was impressed by her courage, standing up to her fear, just to do and share in something that I've loved doing since I was twenty-three years old. We went to Cozumel and sort of fell in love. She loved Mexico and the great diving! Yeah! Welcome to my world baby! I missed it!

    After Lydia and I had first gotten together, the following Monday at school, I couldn't look at Pía. I felt so freaking weird. It was weird. I still had to meet her younger daughter, Cree. I did meet her at five-mile dam one afternoon. She was twelve and looked at me suspiciously. Once Lydia had moved in with me, the girls would show up regularly and shower and eat and stuff there. I didn't mind it at all. It was nice to have some people over. They actually lived across the highway with their father and Lydia's ex. When she moved in she told me that she didn't cook. I thought, *fuck!* So, she let me do all of the cooking for the first month. After coming home late from practice, she decided to surprise me with meat loaf and mashed potatoes. What! You know how to cook? I asked. She said, yes. I never said I didn't know how to cook, just that I didn't cook. It doesn't make sense to cook for one person. That's what I did, as you can see! I taught her to make fideo, but she already was and is an excellent cook. Yes!

    Lydia had to have back surgery that first summer. She had good insurance working for the Statesman. We got to know each other much better. My father had told me that he would be retiring soon. This meant that he would be living at the house in Alice all alone, not a good idea. Near the end of every year, I would go on the TASA website to see where in Texas they have openings for Spanish teachers. Alice I.S.D. actually had two openings. **Confession:** Now let me just say that I never thought that I would ever move back to Alice, TX. But I've heard other people say, you do it for family, which is the only reason I decided to interview and secure a teaching position. After the interview, Lydia and I were driving home. I had interviewed with Mr. Gamez and Ms. Y. I think it was Mr. Gamez who called to offer me the job, which I did accept.

9. A Homecoming?

The house In Alice on Dewey St. was in terrible condition. No one had been living in it for a while. Lydia and I went several weekends to clean and paint the house before we could move in. It was a lot of work. Lydia wanted to move away for a change. I told this would be it for sure. I mean, I love being in Central Texas, but like someone told me, you do it for family. I had to formally ask my father first, if it was OK if I moved back home. Of course he told me that it would be fine. He met and liked Lydia and especially her cooking!

At my new teacher orientation, one of the presenters, Mrs. Halloway was talking about something and Gene, the new Spanish teacher at the Junior High, and later an Assistant Principal at the High School, and I were discussing quietly what was being said by Mrs. Halloway. Well, she gets upset that we're talking. She calls us out and we have to apologize. Shit, I couldn't believe it. What was I getting myself into? **Sidebar:** A couple of years later, at a Teacher's Inservice at the High School, Mrs. Halloway was using my classroom for one of her meetings with other teachers. I had to go to my classroom during a break and walk in. All of the teachers are there and Mrs. Halloway said to me what a nice classroom you have. We love it. I had all kinds of 8 X 10 framed pictures of fish, whale sharks, Mt. Denali, pyramids of Palenque and Tikal, and a bulletin board full of pictures of places that I have traveled to. I don't think she remembered scolding me.

The first place Lydia and I ate after coming to Alice was at the Bowling Alley. We got a couple of burgers. I was excited to go and eat some steak fingers at Dena's Restaurant, now closed. Dairy Burger also had good steak fingers and some excellent hot sauce to go with them. They also served a deluxe burrito. It was deep-fried and served with chili, cheese, onions and Texas toast. Mmm good! There was no shortage of Mexican Food restaurants in Alice. I liked Charros, but the best is Taquería Vallarta. Everything they serve is so good, from the menudo, or breakfast tacos con la tortilla doradita, just the way I like it, along with a refresco de manzanita. Tacos al pastor, migas, carne guisada, I'm making myself hungry now. Let me also add an old school friend from elementary Horacio Lopez had a converted his dad's old Texaco station to Cowboy's, a barbeque restaurant. This is how hardcore he was; he refused to eat the barbeque that was served at our 30th High School Reunion.

About that reunion, it was nice to see everyone, some good friends. I also found all those classmates that have passed away over the years. I hadn't seen some of these people since graduation. Diane, an old friend since 6th grade, we were both in Mr. Serna's homeroom class. Well, she called me over to take a picture with her. Lydia had just stepped outside to have a smoke. Coincidentally, she was out there with Diane's husband who was also having a smoke. So Diane calls me over, then someone else comes and says I want to get in the picture, then another, and another, another. Shit! I didn't want to be taking a pic with all of these women! What you gonna do? I'm in the middle of I don't know how many women and guess who walks in just in time to see all of this, Lydia. I had been invited to a party by an old friend from high school, Polla. It was good to see her and some other of my old friends. I hadn't seen most of them in years. I wanted Lydia to meet them. Everyone was very nice and genuine. I had spent most of the evening chatting with Manny Torres. An old girlfriend of mine was there also. She had married one of my good friends and I wished he would have come as well, but did not. All the while I was there, I had been drinking some Sangría wine. It went down really good. I must have had only three drinks, but it hit me and I felt a little tipsy. It's the only time that Lydia has seen me in this condition. I let her drive home at her insistence. We did get pulled over by a cop on our way home because of a burned out taillight.

At the high school I would be teaching only Spanish 1 for that first year. Well, that's ok, but I can and want to teach more. It wouldn't be until the following year that I would teach level 2. At least I would know that the kids in my class would learn correctly. I saw some people I recognized that I went to school with. I saw Patsy, then I saw what I thought was my fourth-grade teacher. I looked at Patsy who was across the room. I asked her only mouthing, not saying the words. Is that Miss Flowers? I asked. She nodded yes. I then again, mouthed, she was a mean bitch! She smiles and nods yes. I laugh. I couldn't believe that she was still teaching. Looking at her, I felt sorry for her. She was old and still trying to hang on.

The school was bigger, as they added a couple of big wings. It was a class 5-A school. I liked everyone in our department, they all seemed nice enough. I just wanted to do my job well. On my first day of school, I recognized one of my students, just by looking at him. I didn't even know his name, but I called out, Alejandro! He turned around and I asked him his name. He was the son of one of my good buddies from high school, Amado. It just so happened that my stepdaughter Megan and Amado's son were in the same class. I had sent them and a couple of other students to the board to write something. As Megan was writing, Amado's son was next to her and he started leaning towards her, trying to sniff her hair. I yelled out, HEY, hey what the ... He got embarrassed, but so did Cree. It was hard to keep from laughing my ass off!

One of the other teachers, Jorge, was in charge of the Spanish Language Lab. The kids got to put on head phones and talk to each other and do lessons in there. I went to him for many of the questions a new teacher might have. He later got his administrator's degree and moved up and became a real asshole. I've always said, if you want to see how someone really is, give them a little bit of power and their true personality will come out. I've seen it so many times. You can practically predict what they'll do next. He left, and Juan took over the lab. He

A CHICANO SPANISH TEACHER

was the best teacher in our department. I got to speak a lot of Spanish with him as he was from Tampico, Mexico. He eventually got moved to the Jr. High school because of his ESL certification. I think it was a little retribution for something he may have said or implied, I don't know. He was our best teacher and a great resource for our department. Also on the faculty was Coach Cruz, my freshmen football coach. He's the man who made me into a quarterback. I really respected him and it was so nice to see him again. Mr. De La Cruz was hired about a year later as an Assistant Principal. I've known him since my senior year in high school. He was actually doing his student teaching. I also still call him Coach. These men, friends, now co-workers, really knew who I was and respected me as well. That's nice.

Lydia and I enjoy attending Church. We went to St. Joseph's Catholic Church and the priest, Father Peasley made us both feel quite unwelcomed. He talked about how divorced people couldn't partake in Holy Communion. Whaat? No shit man! What a jerk! Lydia and I still got up and got in line for Communion and when I said "Amen" I made him stick the Eucharist in my open mouth, old school. Ha! He's just a man and he's not going to tell me if I can or cannot take Communion. I asked Lydia after Mass if she felt how I did, unwelcomed. For sure, how could we not? Apparently, we weren't the only ones unhappy with Father Peasley. The Vatican had also heard because he got transferred after having lost so many parishioners. He was replaced by Father Grande, an excellent choice! After my father died and they got rid of Peasley we started to attend St. Joseph's once again.

We then went across the tracks to St. Elizabeth's Catholic Church and the same unwelcomed feeling from the Monsignor there. We were quite disappointed. It's funny how I enjoy going to Mass, whereas, when I was a kid and teenager, not so much. I did graduate in the Catholic Church I might add. I went through all of the CCD classes on through my senior year. It was actually fun. Father Carlos, at the time there at St. Joseph's, was a really cool Father. Lydia and I finally found an excellent Church at Our Lady of Guadalupe with Father George, completely opposite of the previous two. Had a good warm feeling all way from the beginning of the service all the way to the end. It was so refreshing! It seemed that I as soon as I got back to Alice, people I or my family knew started dying. I was going to funerals every month or so. One of my students had asked me if was going to go out and "party" for the weekend. I told him, no. I mostly now go to more funerals than parties. Lydia did tell me that she felt that some Hispanic women in the grocery store were giving her dirty looks. She says that they didn't like her because she had taken one of their own, me. There were other Hispanic women who she got on very well with, like Minerva, our neighbor and many others. If my cousin Gina G. was okay with Lydia, then forget about the haters. It was good to reconnect with Gina, I love her too.

During one of the STAAR Testing weeks there was one day that we had the morning off with nothing really to do. I told Coach Peña and Juan to come to my room to watch *The Hangover*. We turned off the lights and laughed our asses off! Its times like that make the day go by much easier. The administrators get a little crazy when it came to the STAAR Test, short for State of Texas Assessment of Academic Readiness. State educators like renaming state exams every so often. They all want to put their mark on it. There was one newly assigned Assistant Principal. She was in charge of making sure the classrooms in our wing were good to go, as far as not having information on walls for the students to use. I had mostly pictures on my wall and she wanted me to cover them up. I was like what? Why? They are just pictures! She didn't want to take any chances. I felt like an idiot covering all of my walls with long sheets of paper!

After Superintendent Barrera left after many years, they hired this one guy name Saul Something. The first time he came to meet our faculty at a meeting, the first thing he did was say that all of the problems at this school were our fault, the teachers! Everyone looked around and couldn't believe it. Shit, was he trying that hard to make friends? It was his Central Office that moved Jorge up to a high position. Coach Barrera was telling me that one day Jorge was having a parent conference with a Spanish speaking parent. They had called Coach in because Jorge couldn't communicate with a parent speaking Spanish. ¡Ni podía hablar español el baboso! This is what he taught! How? I do not know! I guess he could do a great power-point presentation! More than anywhere else that I've taught, I've seen people change into jerks or assholes when they become administrators. I can easily count around five or six who transformed. It's like they think that they're better than everyone else. It's a shame that they have to put people down in order, for some reason to feel good about themselves. These people that changed were both male and female! Let me just say that it wasn't everyone. No, there were indeed some excellent ones. María, for example was a good, caring, person already before she became an administrator, unlike Jorge and the woman who made me cover my pictures. It was a whole bunch of them who got an Ed. D degree that came with the title Dr. Oh please! Miss G. was a hoot to have in our department. I didn't know her too well, but we soon did. Out of the teachers that were left, she was the only one that I felt comfortable confiding with. That was a huge comfort for me. In our department we would help each other out wherever we could. If a teacher had a Dr.'s appointment at 3:00 P.M. whoever could, would cover their class, rather than have them waste a half-day sick or personal leave. It doesn't make sense. It helps to have a supportive principal as well. Melissa Hernandez was my favorite Alice High Principal. She was only there for two years, but was level-headed, smart, and kind. In the eleven and a half years that I was there at least ten or eleven principals in total.

    I used to buy the teachers in our department souvenir t-shirts from Cozumel or one time I bought everyone a Hawaiian shirt that was on sale at J.C. Penney's. When I came back from Peru, I brought them back some coca candy. I should have brought back more!

    The kids were out of control. I asked the teachers, what's wrong with these kids? They were just plain rude, a whole lot of them. But of course, there are some great kids out there too. It just takes a little more time to see who they are. The misbehavers often seek that negative attention, so they're more visible and easier to spot. I did have some super kids.

While I was a teacher for the first few years, we had to evacuate the building and retreat to the Stadium. We had to walk, and it's usually quite warm in Alice almost year-round. We kept getting bomb threats called in. They even sent us home a couple of times. You should have seen all of the parents! They were all lined up ready to pick their kids up. Yeah, at lunch many of the parents bring their kids lunch from all of these fast-food places! I guess many parents everywhere do this.

Christmas vacation was already here. In Alice the weather is usually very hot and humid. We did have a mild summer this year too. Before the students left, I told my classes, I hope you enjoy the snow! There was no indication at that time in the forecast for snow. Lydia and I drove to the valley to spend Christmas with my cousins. It got very cold, and it did indeed snow! I was in Mercedes, TX on the border with Mexico. When we drove home that morning, the landscape looked incredible! There was snow on the palm trees! Who sees that in South Texas? It looked beautiful. We drove back on Hwy 77. I'm glad we drove Pop's Roadmaster because the car was sliding all over the highway in the thick snow. It was over one foot high! As we were driving, Lydia sees a big buck in a snow-covered field. It looks so majestic there, standing with snow on its horns, beautiful! Cree had gone back to San Marcos, thinking there was a better chance for snow there. Wrong! It didn't snow there at all, she missed it. The snow stuck around for several days before it all melted! Lydia, Carlos, Mom and I had a snowball fight in the front yard! What a treat! When we returned to school the kids were all, how did you know?

At the end of one of my observations, Ms. D, was walking to the door and all of a sudden there was all this banging on the wall! It was loud. Ms. D quickly exited my room as I followed her. Miss G. is at her door, getting ready to unlock it because she's coming back from lunch. Ms. V, tells her, what's the meaning of this, all that banging? G looked puzzled and had no idea what she was talking about. Ms. D walks away. I told Miss G. what had happened, all the banging. She said, oh, that was Benjamin, a ghost who used to be a student here at Alice High. She say's he messes with her computer and she tells him to cut it out, she's trying to get some work done and then it stops!

It was a tough school to be a principal at. We had so many in the 11.5 years that I was there. My second year there I was ready to look for a new job. I had sent my résumé to the North Pole, Alaska school district. It's just outside of Fairbanks in the interior. I did a phone interview and was a finalist. They went with another who would be an in-state transfer. I could understand that. The Principal was very gracious and offered to write me a letter of recommendation! I told him no, he didn't have to do that, but thank you very much. I tried never to be too political during my teaching years. I mainly told students to just vote and take part in our democracy as a citizen of this country. I didn't tell them who to vote for. If they ever asked me I would be honest with them and tell them the truth. They already mostly knew who I was and what my values were just by being in my class. One of my senior students asked me if he could ask me some questions that he had been given in his Government class to find out where I stood politically just by my answers. Wayne, the student's teacher, and I had some good political conversations as I also did with Mr. Ryan another Government teacher who was a news correspondent for an online news agency. He was very insightful. Ok, getting back to the questionnaire, he asked me all kinds of questions with at least four or five responses for me to choose from. After he tallied his score, he said, "hey Mr. Morin, you're a liberal radical!" I told him. I know. I could have told you that!

I had never had any of my own children and it was a new experience to have a teenage step-daughter. It was a little rough; I wasn't used to the histrionics someone that age may present. I hated being called, "Cree's mom's boyfriend." We got married March 12, 2005. We have on several occasions, forgotten our anniversary date. For a few years, we thought it was on the fifteenth. Driving back from Oklahoma one time, our anniversary had already passed by a few days, and neither of us had remembered. So I tell her Happy Anniversary to get the jump on her! I had gotten a haircut with Sara. Her place was on East Main Street. As I'm leaving the parking lot, I get in the right lane and quickly check my left lane so that I could change lanes to make a left turn up ahead. As I turn my head back forward, the slow-motion begins. I see a truck right in front of me! There's no way to avoid it and I brace myself for impact. Just then, there's a light blue bubble that envelops the car. When I make impact with truck, I didn't even feel it. When the car came to a stop, I quickly ran out to check on the people in the truck and they were ok. I called Lydia, and she knew already knew that something had happened. That was weird.

We did have to, on a couple of occasions, get into the small towel closet that was in the hallway of the house. There were tornado warnings and you could hear the city sirens going off. We quickly took out all of the towels and shelves and got in. That last time a huge tree limb fell on the car and in the front yard. I could barely open the front door as there was another big limb on the porch.

Although Pop loved Lydia's cooking, he also liked taking us to Taquería Vallarta. It's a great restaurant there in Alice. The food is so good. We would go there all the time. Sometimes he would treat and sometimes we would treat. Pop liked to go to the Regal Beagle, it was a small bar. Lydia had dropped him off there one evening for a little while. Pop loved his brew! When it came time to go and pick him up I sent Lydia and Pía, both blondes. I could see Pop getting all braggadocio since these two blonde women were picking him up and taking him home. Before they left, he had them drink a beer with him. He loved that! Lydia said he was all happy to see them. Yeah, I'm sure he was!

Pop had a stroke in July 21, 2010. He was in the hospital at Spohn in Corpus Christi, then, we brought him home. He couldn't talk or do anything. He had a hemorrhagic stroke. We had gotten a call from H.E.B. that my dad needed some help. They noticed he scribbled his handwriting on a check. I quickly got to the store and saw him in his Suburban. It was hot and he was drenched in sweat, all wet. He looked confused. I told him that I loved him and that we were going to take care of him. The ambulance got there, but they kept him there in the parking lot too damn long! I kept telling them, let's go already! He needs to see a Dr.! They would tell me to let them do their work. I still say they took too fucking long! We brought him home and disconnected the intravenous feeding tube. We had to let him go. He wouldn't have wanted to keep going on in that condition. What kind of a life would it be? It was hard to see him like that. I often cried when I left his room. I would talk to him and also read to him. One of our neighbors had a church deacon come over and sing some songs for him. I really appreciated that. It was a very hard time. Lydia took care of Pop while I was at work. She loved him also as a father. He was the closest thing she had to a father. He died on October 1, 2010. When we called the hospice service they had a hard time getting him out of the room. Then they had a hard time getting him out of the house. When they got to the ambulance, they couldn't put the stretcher in. It wouldn't go in. After a little while, it slid on in. His funeral was at the Guadalupe Church and after the mass we would drive to Orange Grove to the Casa Blanca Cemetery. On the way, in Orange Grove, there's another cemetery with a sign that said turn right. I knew that it wasn't the right turn. My brother was driving and he didn't follow the Hurst. It finally turned around and came back. We got back on track. I think Pop was just having a little fun. In the mornings Pop would usually turn on the coffee pot, being the first one up. The first two days after he died, the coffee pot turned on by itself for those two days after the funeral.

    I was sitting at my desk and I had received an email from Tony, my former student from Junior High. He was a drummer in the band I played with at the Talent Show a few years ago. He was inviting me to his CD release party In Austin. He sent me a CD of his band, "Killing in Apathy." Dang, I couldn't make it being in Alice and all. I really wish that I could have gone, as it was so good to hear from him. A couple of weeks later, he tells me that they would be playing in Corpus at the House of Rock. Great! He also said Brian's band would be playing at Zero's. Brian's band went on first, so Lydia and I went there. Let me tell you, it sure looked like a zero. It was a place to play. When we got there, Brian's band was just setting up. I went up to the stage and asked, where's Brian Harrison? He turned around with his long stringy hair, hey Mr. Morin! He then yells to the audience, this man is responsible for me playing! I said, shut the fuck up! You guys were already good! It was so good to see him! They rocked it out! We then went to the House of Rock on the other side of town. I saw Tony and he introduced me to his girlfriend. We visited before his band was to go on. It was so good to see him. The singer, Mick, was also one of my Junior High students, but I didn't recognize him. He sang screamo, which I usually don't like, unless it's someone that I know personally, like say my cousin Mark G. They rocked it out as well. This was around '08 or '09. I would hear from him again in another ten years!

Alicia, the department chair was retiring. I told my wife that they might offer me the department chair position. I had already mentioned to Coach Peña that if they needed a chair, to consider me. I was the only teacher with a Master's. Well, Lydia and I were in Cozumel, as usual, and she gets a call from the high school on her cell. They ask to speak to me, but I'm somewhere, probably by the pool having a mango tango. They tell Lydia what the call is about, to offer me the department chair position. She tells them that I had told her that I would take it if they offered it. They said that it was good enough for them. I became the new department chair, for the third time in my career.

One of my younger colleagues in his 20's who was a good-looking guy newly married with a newborn baby. Well, there was this was new hire who was twenty-three years old and quite pretty. She was supposedly engaged, but she had told my friend that her fiancé had cheated on her. She was nice and wanted to get together with my friend. Good thing he had dated quite a bit before he got married, don't we all, but he wasn't interested at all. Then one time when we were alone in my classroom, he showed me what she had sent him, a video of herself in the bathroom naked in front of a mirror shaking her ass! Whaaat? It was the first sexting video that I had ever seen. He told me that he had showed it to another buddy, he said, that's the devil! I thought, *you know, he's right!*

I was teaching a unit on agriculture in South America. I was talking about the Quechua speaking peoples of the Andes. I asked them how they were supposed to farm on a mountain. I drew a triangle with no bottom and the point on top, like a mountain. Then, I said, you can't farm on a fucking mountain! I quickly realized what I had said. I stop and look at my class and ask, did I just say that? They all nodded, yes. That was the only time I ever let the "f" word slip out. It's so highly unprofessional to talk like that in front of kids. I had only one coach in all the years of playing sports use profanity. It's so unnecessary and like I said unprofessional. I apologized and they told me it was no big deal. I told them, it was for me! **Confession:** Probably one of the stupidest things I ever did as a teacher was staple a piece of paper to my forehead. Why? I don't freaking know. I knew it wouldn't hurt, but I forgot just how much a little cut on the head bleeds. When I pulled it out, I felt the blood run down my forehead and I quickly leaned forward so that I would not get any blood on my shirt. I did leave my DNA on the carpet though.

A couple of years after she graduated, my step-daughter Cree and her boyfriend had a couple of children, two little girls, Veronica and Carol. As it so often happens, they split up. Neither of them could care for the girls properly. We took them in as our own. We didn't want CPS to take them and put them through any more trauma than they already had. Their parents were both making bad decisions and Lydia and I both felt that we had to protect them. I contacted a lawyer and got custody of them. They were one and two years old at the time they came to live with us. We worked with Veronica because she hadn't yet started talking. Soon enough she did start and hasn't stopped talking yet! They are both very smart people. Way smarter than I was at that age, and I tell them that. Hell, Veronica is my tech support! The girls are still with us and they will be eleven and twelve. I feel like I've prepared all of my life to be at this point where I'm responsible for another person. They both have enriched our lives more than you could know. I count my blessings and thank God for my life!

I was in the audience at a talent show. One of the performers was up there playing air guitar but with an actual guitar. She was just going through the motions with a song that was playing. She was having fun, but I sort of felt bad for her. I'm sure she had to be persuaded to do this. I said, I can play better than that, then, the Art teacher said, I can play better than that too. I asked him, do you play? He said yes, then he asked me, do you play? I said yes. Then I said, let's play something next year, like War Pigs. He says yeah! I thought, great! I bet I can talk the English teacher Sammy into singing. He said sure, I have the range! Great, and the Art teacher had a student who was a drummer. Sammy and the Art teacher are in my classroom talking about the band. We didn't have a bass player though. I walked out of the classroom to go the workroom. On the way, I see Mr. Hendrix, a young Social Studies teacher. I continue, then back up and ask him if he by chance played the bass. He said as a matter of fact, I do. I mean, he's already got the last name, right? I said great! I asked, do you have a minute to stop by my classroom? Do you want to join our band? Yeah, sure! Awesome! I already know most of the song, minus the leads. Dan has already been in bands and had my dream setup. He had a Peavey 6505 Plus and 4X12 Mesa Boogie speaker cab. I taught it to him and we practiced and practiced and then brought Sammy in to help us know where we were in the song with the lyrics. Everyone had learned their parts before we would get together to play. When we finally got together it was great. Mikey, the drummer was very good. He didn't know the song, but learned quickly and ripped it good. The week of the talent show on Monday, Mikey wigs out and says he can't do it. What? Fuck! No way! OK be cool. I then thought of the drum percussion teacher. Maybe he could tell me of a drummer or perhaps, even himself. I found out who the teacher was and called him. I told him the situation. He said he didn't want to encroach on anyone's gig. I told him he wouldn't even be doing that. He had to learn the song. We got together and played the song once and almost nailed it. We played it once more and nailed it. Good enough. We should play "Children of the Grave" also I said. It's easy. We went through it once. We were able to practice early at 7:00 A.M. before school. We played War Pigs once and nailed it, then played Children of the Grave and nailed it. We were ready. I was now in control of the talent show. This way I could play with a band if I wanted. It was so much fun.

The Spanish Club was able to charge for the Talent Show. This first time I was in charge, I charged $1.00 per student. We used the money to go to the PASF Convention in San Antonio. All of the performers did wonderful. We were the last to come on. When they opened the curtains, there was much applause, it felt great. We begin, I can't hear my guitar. I can hear the Art teacher's Mesa Boogie. He's got that huge stack and I have a 112 that is miked through the PA system. Finally, I can hear and almost mess up. I recover. Shit, now I know why all of these musicians say that being on stage is the best. Yeah, afterwards I was so freaking high for two weeks! I messed up a little on the second song, but you couldn't really notice too much. This was so much fun. I was looking forward to doing it again. I did have some certificates printed for all those who performed. The certificates had their name and Winner of the Talent Show. Everyone won! In my mania I was coming up with all these ideas. One that came to fruition was Coyotepalooza. I decided to have a free show for the community. We would invite all performers including Shattered Sun as headliners. It was a heavy metal band from Alice. Roger, the drummer was one of my former students when he was all about the guitar. Another renaissance man, playing all of the instruments! Sofia, our Spanish Club president had been in contact with Felipe, the singer. She was so instrumental in making it all happen. The Club gave them a little donation for their troubles. They were great as were the other performers. I wasn't able to put anything together. I was a little disappointed.

At every school I've taught at, there have always been students that I thought could lose it and go on a shooting rampage, God forbid. Luckily it never happened, although we did prepare for it with

Lockdown drills and such. Miss G. and I had this one student. He was a great kid, football player and nice guy. His friend had suddenly died in a car accident and it really messed him up. He started hanging with some bad people. He and two other guys had pulled up to two men working on a fence in Ben Bolt, a small community near Alice. The two guys pulled a gun and shot the men working on the fence and took their truck and burned it. They all got caught and are now serving a life sentence. Things can change drastically in a split second and alter your life forever!

On a bright note, Sofia, the Spanish Club President, and I worked closely for a couple of years now, arranging shows, going to PASF Conventions in S.A. and studying for AP Exams. This girl was outstanding to say the least. She scored a 5 on her AP Spanish Language Exam. She also asked if she could take the AP Spanish Literature. We didn't offer that class, but I gave her two books to look at as a sort of Independent Study. She scored a 3. After she graduated she came by my house to tell me that she would be going to college in San Antonio and majoring in Spanish. She would be the sixth student that I was aware of that had majored in Spanish. It was so nice of her to stop by to let me know. I can't say enough how fortunate I am to be able to meet such awesome people in my job!

It was the summer of 2015 and I was looking to get out of Alice once again. I noticed that Lockhart High School had an opening for a Spanish teacher. I thought, what the hell, I'll give it a shot. Lydia's mother was living with her two sisters and was beginning to fail in her health. I wanted to move up to Lockhart so that she could be closer to her mother and we could get to Central Texas. I interviewed and I thought it went OK, not my best interview. Well, needless to say that I didn't get the job. That was cool. I already had a lot of years of experience, over thirty, which makes my salary higher than it would for a new teacher. That was fine. I had it easy, very easy in Alice I was teaching AP Spanish and Psychology. Great kids too! I think I only had twelve students before lunch along with two conference periods. That's hard to beat.

A CHICANO SPANISH TEACHER

In November I was browsing the Texas Association of School Administrators (TASA), to see what openings there were across the state. I noticed that Lockhart still had an opening. I immediately emailed the principal. She didn't get back to me for two weeks. I thought Oh well, she just blew me off. No problem. Then, I got an email and she asked me if I could get released from my contract. My heart started thumping, almost like a fight-or-flight situation. I called my wife and she told me that I had better not be fucking around. I told her, no, really, that they wanted me to come in again to interview. I could not f'ing believe it. We drove to Lockhart for the interview. They had no one else. I figured the kids had probably run the teacher off, I was right.

Back home we started packing. It was my last two weeks of school in December, just before the Christmas Holiday. It took us two weeks to pack everything to move. We had to be out fast. I feel bad because my mother and Carlos had to go back to Alice on the weekends to clean up after us. They live in Houston. I will always be grateful to them for doing that. I had to find a replacement teacher for my classes. It just so happened that one of our Spanish teachers was doing an internship in counseling. She was in charge of the STAAR test. She didn't really like it and agreed to take my classes. Mil gracias, Michele.

10. Final Assignment

It was a cold December night just after Christmas Day when we arrived in Lockhart. We got a hotel for the night and would move in the following morning. First, we would go and eat at the Dairy Queen. The air felt much lighter now that we were here and I can tell you that the food tasted especially good and the service was great. It was all elderly people that worked there. I think that they make the best employees. We all were excited to be there in Lockhart. I had been ready to get out of Alice two years after I got there. I was there for eleven and a half years. I was ready for something new. I would be teaching Spanish 1 and Spanish 2.

Two days after we got to Lockhart, Little Nanny, Lydia's mother fell and broke her hip. Oh no! We just got here! She would have to undergo several surgeries. I couldn't believe that happened. It got more difficult for Lydia's sisters who her mother was living with. Lydia would also pitch in to help when she could.

When moving to a new school district, a teacher has to learn their system and how they do things. Every school is different. Here in Lockhart I.S.D. they use Google Classroom for teaching. I guess I'm just old school and like to teach the "old fashioned" way, in front of the class using a dry erase or chalk board. At this point in my teaching career I felt that I could handle anything that came my way, but I was not ready for this. I was excited and one of the Vice-Principals introduced me to the class. I introduced myself and he left. I started interacting with the students asking and answering questions. It seemed like an OK class, but then this one boy would not be quiet so that I could continue. I thought to myself, I'll talk to him privately outside, so I asked him to come outside with me for a moment. Shit, he fucking went berserk. I don't know what happened. He got up and started yelling and flailing around. I called the office and several administrators ran to my portable building classroom. I looked at them and shrugged my shoulders. I told them that all I did was ask him to come outside so that I could talk to him privately. I soon learned that the teacher they had hired in August went to lunch and never returned to class! It turned out that my first class was probably the better behaved of all of my classes. In the next class there were a few football players. A couple of them thought that they were all that, maybe for Lockhart. I reached out to the coach by email to see if he could help out by talking to them. He never even responded. What an asshole. I did meet one of the football player's grandparents and she only spoke in Spanish telling me "No hace caso." He doesn't mind. Muy mal educado. Bad manners. I don't know what's wrong with some of these kids. Their parents or grandparents give them everything and they're still such assholes!

  I taught three classes at the High School in the morning and four classes at the Cisneros Freshman Center after lunch. When I drove to the freshmen campus, it looked the same. It was a dark red brick building that was the first high school, then a Jr. High when I was last there in the mid 90's. As I walked into the office, one of the women working there asked me, "Hey, Mr. Morin, Do you recognize these guys?" They were two custodians, Dane, a very tall guy. I recognized him immediately. The other guy was Aaron, I didn't recognize him as quickly but I soon did. I love those guys! Most custodians, I have found, are some of the most awesome people around.

  At the Freshmen Center the kids were climbing the fucking walls! The first day seemed to be normal. The students responded normally, but then it got very difficult. The students were rude as hell. I hadn't ever heard so much cussing out loud. The students would threaten each other and the Administration was not supportive at all. It was like a learned helplessness that I saw in teachers. I came in the middle of the year and the students had not had a teacher all semester. There was a real good substitute teacher, Mrs. Gonzalez, a real jewel. She bore the brunt of the teaching for the Spanish classes. The kids were horrible. She told me they had written in mud on the dry erase board a bunch of obscenities. As far as I'm concerned, they don't pay that lady enough! I decided that I had to review everything and trying to see where the class was academically. I also decided that I would give them a clean slate and remove all of the zeros they had received prior to my arrival. I would have to give them a semester final, as grades were due in early January. The Principal, told me to create a ten question test. I thought, What? My normal semester exams were one hundred items or at least fifty items. I would have to make the easiest semester exam ever. I thought that it wasn't fair to the students that they didn't have a teacher. I mean, it was really some of their fault, the students who would not behave. I'm sure they gave the teacher that I replaced hell. So, I would take that semester exam grade and use it to fill in for the zeros. I thought that would be fair. I think I had only one student who didn't pass the semester. I tried. After saying this, let me tell you that in the year and a half that I was in Lockhart, I gave more zeros in that time than in thirty-three years of teaching combined. I had never seen anything like it. The following year, our Department Chair said not to pass them and not to cut them any slack, so I didn't. It wasn't long before I couldn't wait for Spring Break. I needed it so badly. I had a very difficult time trying to teach. I wanted to be here dammit and no one was going to force me out! I had quite a lot of students as well. I remember, the first time that it rained. No one was in class. I thought, "What the fu…? Since, I was in a portable building and not part of the main building students had to walk outside to get to my classroom. They were allowed not to come to class and would go to the cafeteria when it rained. (I caught myself praying for rain). This was fine by me as it was a break for me. I didn't have to teach, just take roll. Sometimes I would give them a handout if they looked bored. There were two halfway decent classes at the Freshmen Center. In one class they had asked me if I had any dogs. I told them that I had to send my two huskies, Kimo and Kono to a Husky Rescue. I started to get a little emotional and had to walk out of my classroom to try and regain my composure. When I came back inside, I tried to continue but I couldn't hold it together and one boy student came to me and gave me a hug. The whole class got up to give me a group hug. I had never broken down in tears in a classroom! It did make me feel good though. It's a happy story. Kono had to have a knee replacement on both knees and was sent to the University of Colorado in Boulder to do the surgery pro-bono. They would be staying with a foster family who would probably end up adopting them. They were good dogs too. I could not bring them with me to Lockhart as my landlord did not allow any pets what so ever. I'm happy that Kono got the surgery because the vet in Alice said that he had arthritis and we would not have found out and Kono would have suffered more. I've never left or surrendered a pet.

    I used to take pride that I had not written a discipline referral form in years. I never liked to. I promised myself that I would not write one this year either. It was hard, very hard not to. Some kid would do something, and a teacher would say "write 'em up." I had my observation and got my contract renewed. I wasn't sure if they were going to renew it. I had never doubted it before. I did make it to Spring Break and then the end of the year. At the High School I had a couple of decent classes. I decided to buy them some donuts one day. My wife Lydia, brought them over to my classes. If there were any left, I always took them to the office. About a week before school was out, we had to get all of the grades in for the seniors. I didn't even think about it. I was in the shed adjusting my attitude after what I'm sure was a long day, when I remembered a conversation that I had with one of my students. I could remember him telling me what he was going to do after graduation. Then, it clicked that he WAS indeed a senior and that I had not input his grade. Shit! I ran inside to my computer and turned it on. As I'm doing this, the doorbell rings. It was Mrs. Rainy! She came personally to let me know that I had not input that grade. I invited her inside and asked her to follow me to the den where I had my computer. I had known Marian since my Junior High days. She was also the sister of my neighbor Zeke. He said that they didn't get along too well. Anyway, I told her that I was doing just that. As I tried to input the grade, I was having trouble and could not because it was locked. She called to the school and they unlocked it so that I could input the grade. I was so embarrassed and apologized. She didn't seem too worried, but you never know with some people.

I did have something to look forward to this summer of 2016, a trip to Cozumel. We would take both grand-daughters and Carlos and my mom would join Lydia and I. We did have a good time. That was the last time I went to Cozumel. I'm not sure when it will be safe again to travel. I know people still go but, most of the world is still not vaccinated.

Well, the past semester had been the most difficult of my career. I figured it was harder since I came in during mid-year. And now I would have a fresh start. I had been well rested. My neighbor Zeke told us to feel free to come by and swim in his pool while they were at working during the day. What a guy! His backyard was perfectly shaded. It was so cool of him to let us. He made us feel quite welcomed. I would be indebted to him for his kindness.

After returning from Cozumel, I was ready for the next school year. This year I would be inside the buildings but, I would still have to travel to two campuses. At the beginning of every school year the district has a big teacher meeting where all of the teachers in the district meet together and usually get a pep talk from the Superintendent. Teachers go through what seems like a "gauntlet" of insurance agents, 403 B investors, Banks and other businesses trying to get the new recruits set up for whatever. As I was going through one of the lines, this gentleman recognized me and said "Hey! Mr. Morín! I've been looking for you everywhere! I slowly started to recognize him, it was a former Junior High student, Marco De Franco. He told me that I was one of his favorite teachers ever. That's so nice to hear. You know, as a teacher I've been very fortunate to have met such excellent and high-quality people. He was surely one of them. He was now a local bank Vice-President. What a badass! I would later contact him to see if he could come in to my class as a guest speaker. He came to both campuses, what a guy! He was playing to a tough crowd and did a great job.

A CHICANO SPANISH TEACHER

This year I would be in the new building, however I would be sharing a room with an English teacher. I forget his name. He was like me, in that we had to both go to the Freshmen Center. He would go in the morning while I was in his room at the high school. I would go to the Freshmen Center again in the afternoon this year. I had only enough time to eat and rest for a few minutes. This was because I would leave campus during my conference period, it was before lunch. I would stay on campus if I needed to. At the Freshmen Center I would be in the building, one room down from my old room during my Junior High days. Mrs. Liguez, an English teacher now taught in there.

Our Principal at the Freshmen Center was going to be Ms. Wesley, but she decided to take another job at Lehman High School in Kyle as Principal there. This left us with no principal. We did have an Assistant Principal Mrs. J. I didn't want to misspell her name. She was a tall, thin, good-looking black woman. I really relied on her quite a bit throughout the year. I had to call her office often to send disruptive students there. She already knew when I would call. I feel bad for her. All the Admin. had to do is remove the disruptive students so that the teachers can teach, but that did not happen here. She was a big help though.

All of the teachers were supportive of each other as usual. The teachers at the Freshmen Center told me that it didn't do any good to write referrals because nothing would happen. They would send the kid more often than not, back to the classroom! The kid comes back and says, "See I told you they weren't going to do anything," with a stupid smirk on their face that you wish sometimes that …that they would be nicer. As always there are hidden gems in the student body. In every place that I've taught I have had some of the most awesome students, just plain good people. The new Spanish teacher the district hired to teach at the Freshmen Center told me a few months into the year, that he would take a 10K pay cut, to have a better-behaving group of kids. I told him, yeah, me too! Seriously, I would have, it was that bad!

At the Freshmen Center the Counselor had asked me if I could grade some of the Spanish Placement Exams. They were all essays.

She told me all I had to do was decide if she wrote good enough to go into Spanish 3. I figured no problem. I'm too fucking nice sometimes and get suckered in. Well, there were about thirty-seven or thirty-eight exams that I felt were good enough. They had used quite a bit of the Subjunctive Mood since many were true native speakers. I was teaching Spanish 1, Spanish 2 and Spanish 2 Pre-AP. Can you guess what happened next? Yes, the counselor asked me if I would kindly volunteer to teach a Spanish 3 class to the freshmen. Now the way I am, I had always chosen to teach more when I could. So what did I agree to? ¡Pendejo! I told her that I would. I was making more work for myself. I thought great, I would at least be speaking more Spanish, if not completely. They put all of those kids in my class. All thirty-eight of them! Those bastards! My total enrollment of students in all of my classes was going up. They would be putting kids in my other classes as well. At first the Spanish 3 class was fine. Kids were paying attention and doing their work. There were a couple of kids that would not stop talking or do any work at all. I complained to the counselor and she wouldn't move on it. We didn't have a principal for a while until we got an interim Principal. He was coming from the Junior High School. I guess he was doing such a great job there. When he arrived, I went to him and they took two of those kids out. I still had too many that didn't need to be there. There were about fifteen students that I could work with, but they only took out ten more. Well, that's better than nothing, I guess. I mean, where are they going to put them?

 I was to have my observation there at the Freshmen Center. Ms. J. would be doing it. I would rather do it there anyway. My original date had to be postponed, I can't remember why. I chose for her to come into my Spanish 3 class. She could see us interacting completely in Spanish. When she showed up, some of the students were being uncooperative and I had very little participation. I only had a couple of students answering stuff. I was really pissed. I started telling them that I guess that I was a terrible teacher for them not to pay any attention to me. I told them that this class was easy for them. They didn't want to do the work. I mean, they were only freshmen and it was an advanced class. Many of them were immature. I said that I was disappointed that the principal had to see this. My worst observation EVER! About a week later, Mr. Jones called me into his office. He told me that some students had complained about me. He said that I spoke to them in an ugly manner and that I was discouraging them. WHAT? I told him that I never discouraged them, but that they had a great opportunity to get ahead in Spanish and possibly take an AP class for college credit. Who was I kidding? Only thirty-four percent of Lockhart graduates went to college at that time. I told him that I was more self-deprecating than anything. He already had a form for me to sign. He wrote me a fucking referral! I could not believe it! He did this because a student or students complained and before he had even listened to me, the teacher. He must have already known the students from their Junior High days so he believed them. I signed the damn paper, I didn't care. That was the first time I had ever been written up. This would not be the last time I'd be in his office. The following Monday, I did apologize to the Spanish 3 class telling them that I didn't mean to offend anyone and if I did that I was sincerely sorry. I had to hold the students accountable for their grades. Many of those Freshmen students were failing. I did not drop any zeros. Mr. Jones told me that I could allow them to correct their exams to help them pass. He said that his college professors did that for his classes. I'm thinking, *when the fuck did you go to college?*

It was a Tuesday after school. The bell rang and there was an announcement that there would be a mandatory faculty meeting. I was so freaking tired! I ran out of my vitamin B 100 for the past two days and I was dragging. I climbed the stairs to the second floor and made my way to the library. The Assistant Superintendent greeted everyone, she said, Hi, How are you? I said tired. Well, they get the meeting going and they start saying that Mr. Jones was being promoted to Central Office as an Assistant Superintendent. It was a freaking pep rally for Mr. Jones! I couldn't believe it. I guess he did a great job the short time he was there at the Freshmen Center. The Superintendent started talking about this and that and when she asked, are there any questions? I raised my hand in what felt like slow-motion. I said Yes, when are you going to hire more teachers? I caught her off guard. She said, well, well, ugh, we just hired some. *Yeah, for a new school,* I said to myself. I said I have over two hundred students. I have to come to work early two hours every day, and come in on Saturdays and Sundays just to get some work done. Then I said I don't even really like being a teacher anymore. Then the Assistant Superintendent said, maybe you shouldn't. I thought, right. I fucking rained on his parade! Normally, I would not say a word in a faculty meeting. Everyone wants to get the hell out of there. I got some looks from some of the teachers. I do regret saying that though. The following day a couple of the teachers came up to me and thanked me for saying what I did. Thanks alot assholes for not backing me up! They are all scared of losing their jobs. The counselor's secretary, a very nice older black lady told me when I went into the office, "Oh, Mr. Morin you were scaring me with what you were saying." I told her that I had to say something that this was not normal. By now I knew that I would probably be leaning more to retire at the end of the school year."

Back at the High School campus on the first or second day of school there was a fight. I later found out that it was one of my former students from the previous year. He had gotten pummeled by another student very badly and needed to go to the hospital. Nothing ever happened to the kid that beat him up, nothing. They had it on camera, so there was no dispute as to what had happened. The Central Office decided that they would not suspend the kid, why? I don't know. Superintendent Garza had no experience in the classroom and was a lawyer, someone later told me. They had just hired one of her friends as Assistant Superintendent. Those were the two women that I addressed at Mr. Jones's pep rally.

On our first staff development we spent all day learning and practicing about how to "engage" students. What? I have been doing this for over thirty years! Really? Most of the teachers took this seriously and really got into it. I could not believe it. A couple of the teachers were in the same camp as I. It was embarrassing and humiliating. I don't know.

A CHICANO SPANISH TEACHER

In my first morning class there was a group of students that would bring tacos and drinks to class almost every day. It was not permitted and they knew it. One morning, there were some kids in the back and a soda got spilled on the floor. I went over to them and was going to tell them that this was the reason why we didn't allow food or drinks in class. I walked over and only got out "This" when all of a sudden the girl stood up and yelled out loudly, FUCK OFF! This was in my classroom! I asked her why are you talking to me like this. When at the same time this other female Hispanic student got up and yelled "YOU FUCKING BITCH YOU CAN'T TALK TO HIM LIKE THAT! She told me tell her Mr. Morin, tell her. I had to get in between both of them to keep them from fighting. It was freaking pandemonium! No one had ever spoken to me like this. The girl that yelled at me left the class. Yeah, students would walk out whenever they wanted to. Many didn't give a damn. The kids would say, just let 'em go Mr. Morin. I went to the Counselor's Office to get that girl out of my class. This was a first for me. I had never kicked a kid out of my class. I had to write a paper documenting the incident. I would be steadfast and be firm on this. I asked the Counselor why was she even in my class since she already had all of her language requirements. And do you know what she told me? Oh, we don't tell the students what classes to take. We let them choose. I'm thinking, *well what the fuck good are you doing as a Guidance Counselor?* I couldn't believe it. I could tell that the Principal, Ms. Pérez was not pleased. I didn't give a shit. What are the students to think if that girl returned to class with nothing happening to her? No it was not happening, not this time. I had to talk to an Assistant Principal. He had gotten demoted from Central Office as Assistant Superintendent. I don't know what happened there. I explained to him what had happened. I told him that the school was pretty fucked up. He agreed. He said that the kid that had gotten beat up was really messed up. The Number 1 and Number 2 didn't want to do anything about it. It didn't matter to him. I told him that if it was my child, I would sue the hell out of the district and Superintendent. I could tell he was ready to get out and he soon did.

There was no warmth or compassion coming from Central. It was mostly like that. For example, even before my self-expression at that prior meeting, I had met with my Principal Ms. Pérez. I told her that I was feeling overwhelmed with all of the students I had. I mentioned that they did take out about ten students from class at the Freshman Center, but I still had too many. I even had a very, very difficult time remembering all of my students. One morning, I could not remember this one girl's name, and she shouted out her name and asked me if I was ever going to learn it. She was right. I never did forget *her* name though. What used to take me a couple of days now took weeks. But then again, I didn't have as many students. Something around one-hundred and twenty students or so is much more manageable and normal. I was teaching in one of the poorest counties in Texas. They need good attendance so that they can get money from the State.

I talked to my Dept. Chair, Bernadette about how I was feeling. She told me that Ms. Pérez had come to her and asked, "What's wrong with Sonny?" She had reiterated that I had too many students. I was even losing sleep. I woke up several times in the middle of the night and could not go back to sleep. I could see the street light come through a crack in the curtain. I knew that I would soon be getting ready for class. It was a dreadful feeling. A couple of times when I had gone to school after not sleeping, I mentioned it to Bernadette and she told me that she also had trouble sleeping. She was with child and I could tell that she was indeed tired as well. She still glowed with life even though she felt as tired as she did. She was a big comfort to me. Our classrooms were next door to each other. She was also a roaming teacher who had to go to the Junior High campus to teach German. She was going to be returning the following year. I hope they treated her right.

I had a couple of terrible walk-through observations by the assistant principals. One principal came in and I was showing a Gabriel Iglesias video. He started talking about getting drunk before attending his tenth graduation anniversary and what he said once he got introduced. It was hilarious, but I should have turned it off shortly after he entered. The assistant principal told me that he could write

A CHICANO SPANISH TEACHER

me up, but he would give me another opportunity or a walk-through. I thanked him. He was really a nice guy and he got taken advantage of by his superiors. I believe he stayed one more year after I had left.

Another walk-through was done by a newly hired female and a former Spanish teacher herself. Whoopsy freaking do! It was a beginning Spanish class and I was explaining how stem-changing verbs worked. After class she told me that the AP Spanish Exam no longer included grammar, which I knew. What, did she want me to pass out some of Jorge Luis Borjes novels. How about García Marquez? Give me a freaking break! No one in the department liked her. I think they all got together and told her not to tell them how to teach. This was the year after I left as I later found out. She too left soon. It was an exhausting year with too many students and not enough support from the administration. It was no longer fun and I could not wait for the year to be over and done with. I did take my students at the Freshmen Center out to the courtyard to do some oral exercises. The Principal Mr. Castillo quickly asked me if I had it written in my lesson plans to go outside. I said, No, but it's a beautiful day! He didn't like that. In his mind, he's probably thinking too much can go wrong. He was a big control freak. He came in telling us he had fifteen years of experience and was a former wrestling coach. He was a big guy and tried to be soft-spoken. I could barely hear him speak at the faculty meetings. He called me in because some kid told him that I had hit him with a piece of paper! I let one sheet of paper lightly cover his head! What? Yeah, I did it. The kid wasn't paying attention and I was telling him if he did he would know what I was talking about. Another kid got in my face and started yelling at me. I stood my ground and told him that I didn't argue with minors! That threw him for a loop. He responds, I'm not a minor. I was thinking, *yeah, that's why I called your mother during class when you were misbehaving, right?* He would act right for two days or so, then back to his 'ole assholey self. Apparently some of these kids who don't know how to act civilized are calling the shots. One administrator I would see walking with these little shits, three or four of them. They would just walk where ever they wanted to with the

Administrator following. I had some of these kids. I couldn't believe it! Shit, get me the fuck out! I persevered and turned in my letter of resignation. This experience left a bad taste in my mouth. It's too bad that it had overshadowed the bright spots that are the great students that were in my classes despite some of their idiot classmates.

I parked my car on June 2, 2017 and that was the last time I drove a car. It was a relief knowing that I would not have to teach in Lockhart anymore. I feel bad for the good teachers here, because there are some very good ones, for the admins lack of support. I did see one of my former colleagues one Sunday morning at a local restaurant. She told me that Castillo had been moved up to the high school as principal. He was named Principal and Ms. Pérez could go back to the elementary school level. She told me that I had gotten out just in time. She said that they tried to make the teachers feel like all the problems were because of the teachers. What a load of BS! That's not the first time I've heard that.

Well, I did get black-balled and could not get hired even as a substitute! Like I said, they hired my wife with zero college hours and I have a Master's! You know I wouldn't want to work for a district like that anyway! The good thing about retiring is that I would now be able to afford to get my wife on my insurance with Teachers Retirement System (TRS). It would be finally more affordable. I would be able to get her on in September of 2017. I did in fact get her on finally. She was now able to see a Dr. Then, in January when I got my paycheck, I noticed that it was short by a little over $500! What the…? My insurance had gone up. Apparently the Texas Republican Legislature voted to use the retired teachers of Texas to balance their budget! Why don't people vote these bums out? People are already on a fixed income and they still choose to do what they did. I can't freaking believe it! It really ticks me off! I finally was able to get my wife on my insurance only to have me cancel it since I can't afford the new rates. She had insurance from September in 2017 to March of 2018. She hasn't had insurance since then. What a miserable shame, how we are treated. That's Abbott's Texas, #1 in the country in uninsured citizens!

11. Changes

In December of 2017 I was able to get a pair of eSight glasses. I went to Austin for a demonstration and long story short, they did help me see better. The assistant had me read a card. I did with ease. I hadn't read anything in a while and I missed not being able to read. It helps me more to reverse the contrast, where the lettering is white and the background is black. The glasses were very expensive, $10K! I was able to get a grant to pay for part of it, four thousand, and I would have to come up with the rest. My mother was adamant in me getting those glasses. She and Carlos would give me two thousand and her cousin, Marie would match that, leaving me with two thousand to pay. We were able to get the money together quickly. A couple of weeks after I had gotten them, I accidently dropped the unit and part of it broke and would not function. I did call my representative and they promptly sent me another pair! Unfortunately, now in 2021, they are not as effective, if any, at all. The letters and magnification don't work for me as well anymore. Even, with the eSight glasses, I knew that I would need some kind help and or training.

In the meantime, Lydia and I would walk the girls to school every day. In Lockhart, they do not have any flashing school zone lights, except on State Hwy 142. Cars would regularly speed on through the school zones and crosswalks. I almost got hit a couple of times by cars very early in the morning. My wife Lydia, went to the Central Office to see if they could get school lights installed. No luck. They told her that it was the city's responsibility. What pisses me off is when they say that "the safety of the children is what is most important." What line of BS! They don't give a shit. Lydia even walked over to the mayor's house to see if he could do something. Same thing, the city doesn't have the money. But, they did have the money to spend thousands to fix up the football stadium and put artificial turf on it. You would think that the football team makes the playoffs every year! Nope. One afternoon while Lydia and I were waiting for the girls outside the school for the bell to ring, we were talking about the stadium and what a waste of money it was. Some young parent waiting there too, chimed in and told me that football scouts don't want to come to a ghetto stadium. I'm thinking, *they go to see talent, end of story.* As if they gave a damn what the stadium looks like. It's not a well-educated population in general.

We often had a hard time with Veronica not wanting to go to school, because of the atmosphere in her classes. She was getting bullied and no one was doing anything about it. She did have some good teachers. Mrs. Floyd was the best out of all of them. She cared and it showed. Veronica wouldn't let go of us sometimes. It broke our hearts. I knew that I didn't want them in this school district anymore.

I went to the Texas Workforce Commission in Austin to see about getting some help with my job search. It was going on two years of me telling myself that I had skills. I stayed as busy as possible, mostly doing the mowing in my yard. Let me tell you, it was a corner lot and there was quite a bit to mow. I also had to mow outside of the fence. It was where kids would walk to and from school, so I liked to keep it cut. Other than that, emptying the dishwasher and ice trays and helping out with the laundry and vacuuming. It still left me too much time to watch politics on TV. It was breaking news every fucking minute! It was exhausting!

It was August when I took a cab from Lockhart to Austin. My TWC counselor sent one for me so that I could meet with her. When I got dropped off, it wasn't by the front entrance so I had to walk around looking for it. I called my counselor and told her I was in the vicinity and was looking for her office. I was already running late since my ride was late in picking me up. This was the wake-up call I needed to go to the Criss Cole Rehabilitation Center there in Austin.

A CHICANO SPANISH TEACHER

My counselor had been trying to talk me into going for some time now. I didn't want to since I would be essentially living there at the Center, except on the weekends. I knew that I needed some training. I did not use a cane at that point. People assume you can see if you don't have anything to identify yourself as a blind person. I wanted to get in by October, but it wasn't until January 6 when I first got there. I had gone for a day visit to CCRC for a tour. Everyone was super nice and I felt very comfortable. I had to get all of my ducks in line in regards to my paperwork to be able to attend. Finally, it was all set. My wife and granddaughters drove me to Austin. We unloaded all of my stuff and Lydia saw where I would be living and met my roommate, Craig. It was hard saying goodbye to everyone, but I knew that I had to do this. It was such a great opportunity for me to learn and possibly, network some. That very first night we had a meeting and then we had to watch a video on sexually transmitted diseases. What? I wasn't planning on fucking anyone! We were in close quarters with everyone. It was like a co-ed dorm. Yeah, maybe some people needed to watch that, not me! I was there for something other than that! I did cut my long hair before I left for CCRC. It was to the middle of my back. Short hair would be much easier to care for and less maintenance. The residence hall director, Miss Tina, would go in and check to see if the newbies knew how to make their beds. Everyone was saying that she would make them mess up their beds, and make it back up. She had done almost everyone and I was one of the last ones. When she came in she saw that my bed was already made, nice and neat. She didn't make me undo it. I told her that I always made my bed anyway, so it was no big deal. She asked me to show her how I swept with a broom. I told her that it was kind of hard because I couldn't see what I was sweeping. She then showed me how to do it by sweeping a small area to the trash can, then moving the trash can a bit and repeat. Oh, that was easy. Why didn't I think of that? Miss Tina was a slender, strong and very attractive woman. I made sure to give her a hug before I left. I really appreciated her allowing me to use the phone every evening to call my wife. I didn't have a phone. At that point, I had never had a smart phone, only dumb ones. This was in 2019!

I liked my roommate Craig since we were similar in age. I was fifty-eight and he was fifty-four. It turned out that he had also gone to Hill Junior College, we were both Rebels! He gave me so much valuable information. He let me know that I would be able to get all of my books for free using the BARD app on my phone. It made my eyes water to know that I would be able to get books, ebooks that I could listen to at my convenience. When I became a member of the Talking Book Club (TBC) they sent me a recorder with three tapes that had three books each on each tape! I listened to the whole twenty-nine hours of Herodatus' travels and on the ancient civilizations of the Mediterranean. I had never even heard of Gilgamesh! It was great!

The following morning our Orientation and Mobility (O&M) teacher, Daisy drove about five of us guys to downtown Austin to the Capital Metro Office to get our I.D. cards so that we could ride the bus and get a discount for being disabled. Yeah, I finally got my hearing tested, and yes, I'm fucking deaf too. It seems that my mother was right in telling me that I was going to go deaf when she walked into the house and I had Grand Funk on the stereo on maximum volume blasting out "We're An American Band"! I had moderate to profound hearing loss in both ears! I would be getting some hearing aids, but I would not get them until April.

There were thirteen of us that came in at the same time to CCRC. We had a good group. I met Adan, he lived up the road from me near Mustang Ridge. I would be getting a ride with him, as his wife drove us back to Austin. My wife Lydia grew up in Austin, but it's not the way it used to be. It's insane now, the traffic. She absolutely hates it, driving in Austin. Shit, I'm glad that I don't have to deal with it anymore. Hell, I used to do all of the driving! Things change, ¿no? I really did enjoy that first week. I remember laughing all the time and felt that I was with "mi gente, my people" finally. They understood more than anyone what I was going through. At first, we all sat in the cafeteria with people in the same group we came in with. We all wore our mind fold masks, except in the cafeteria. One day that first week we were all getting used to doing things a little differently, like carrying a tray. When I finished my breakfast, I got up to return my tray to the window where we would put our dirty trays and dishes. As I walked by my table, I dropped my cup. I asked my new friends if they could help me get it from under the table. Well, you can imagine six or so blind people looking for a transparent plastic cup! It was freaking hilarious! I had to call George, the head guy, to come get the cup for me. We all had a good laugh!

People there at CCRC had all kinds of eye afflictions. Many had Retinitis Pigmentosa, Glaucoma, Macular Degeneration, even eye trauma from automobile accidents. My counselor and one of my teachers were completely blind. You know the saying, "The blind leading the blind?" Well, it works here at CCRC. They could get around better than me in that building! I still think that compared to many students there, I still had a good amount of vision.

That first six weeks I had orientation and mobility or O&M, Technology, Adaptive Skills, and Industrial Arts. I liked all of my teachers, well at first. Students were saying that I was going to put on twenty pounds, since the food was so good in the cafeteria, and it was! No, I couldn't put on that much weight. I vowed to lose weight and when I left, I had lost twenty pounds, mostly by walking during my O&M class with Daisy! She would show me how to use the cane and how to maneuver the bus system in Austin, blindfolded! It takes quite a bit of concentration. You have to listen carefully to all of the sounds. I couldn't do that without my hearing aids, so I was a bit limited with what I could do. We walked everywhere. I was able to go to the different bus stops and take a bus to where I needed. Pretty soon I was able to have conversations on the bus with the different students that I knew. I could recognize their voices. We would talk to the bus drivers and let them know where we needed to be dropped off, as to give them a heads up. Central Austin is very blind friendly since this is where CCRC is and also the Texas School For the Blind. The further away you move from the center of town the less friendly it gets. What

I have found is that most people are indeed good. I often got help in doing my assignment from bystanders. It seemed that I was wondering around the Wal-Mart parking lot. I had to find the sidewalk and I would be good. All of a sudden, an elderly woman asked me if I needed any help. I told her that I needed to find the sidewalk; it led to the bus stop. I've already created these mental maps of where I was. She asked me if she could walk me to the bus stop. I told her that it wasn't necessary since she led me to the sidewalk. She said, please, my son is also blind I feel that by helping you, someone is helping him. Shit, I almost felt like crying, but surprisingly I didn't and gladly accepted her invitation to escort me to the bus stop. There are so many stories. I had to find the Starbucks at the UT campus. I cross the street from a little way down from where the bus drops us off. You have to go up two or three flights of steps. It helps to ask questions or get a little help. I heard someone speaking and asked where the Starbucks was. He said straight ahead to the left up the stairs. I found it. On the way back to the bus stop, someone yelled out to me, "Hey buddy you've got stairs about ten feet ahead." Thanks man. I was proud of myself when I accomplished my goal. I saw it as adventure. I had to meet Miss Daisy at the bus stop and I got turned around at our entrance and couldn't find the sidewalk. Fuck! I kept trying and trying and in my frustration, took off my mask to get my bearings and immediately put it on. That was the only time I cheated, so to speak. I had a hard time at first walking in a straight line. I kept veering to the left. Our assignments in O&M at first were indoors, like trying to find all of the fire exits in the building, upstairs, downstairs and in the gym. Or tell everything that is in the snack room, only by feeling with our hands. Adan was so good at this. He had very good bearings. Me, on the other hand was told that I don't have good spatial awareness. I usually have a tune in my head. It was hard not to be swaying my head around like Stevie Wonder. Really, I was quite happy to be there.

  I had Adaptive Skills with Miss -Cisco. She was so nice. She taught me brail in four days. By Thursday I knew brail. Earlier in the week, Craig, explained the concept to me and I quickly understood.

It was so exciting! Miss Sarah also helped me to understand brail. I had to feel if it was thicker on top or below and that gave me the clarification I needed to understand. I did have a little neuropathy in part of my right index finger, which made feeling a little more difficult. My finger is now numb; I call it my "dead finger."

That first weekend home I was ecstatic! I spoke with my mother on the phone and told her of my time there. It was very emotional. I was like trying to laugh and cry at the same time. I think I freaked out my grand-daughter a little bit. But I had so much hope now. They would help give me the tools and information I needed as a new blind person. While there on the weekends I would catch up on the mowing and whatever else we needed to do like putting up the swimming pool or going somewhere. The weekends always went by pretty fast.

I did make contact with Tony, a former student of mine. He now had his own club and had been trying to get me to his club, Come and Take It Live, since I got to Lockhart. I invited a few friends to go and catch a show. It was so cool. When I got to the club, the crew asked me if I was Tony's teacher. I said "yes," and they gave me the royal treatment. He put us in the skybox right over the stage. It was freaking great! It was so, so good to see Anthony and meet his crew. Casey, worked the door taking fees and putting bracelets on customers, etc. She was so cool, they all were. It was like they were all family and Tony is one very cool dude. It's nice to see him thriving in his element. I spoke to him on email and he was managing a group and was on the Korn tour with them. I worry about him because of COVID. I caught a few shows between February and June. It was so nice to be able to have a little independence. It was nice being able to take a Metro Access to places like the club or anywhere else they go in the city.

Miss Cisco had a full-stocked kitchen to help learn or adapt to cooking blind. I can already cook, I just haven't in a while since my wife, Lydia, is a great cook. I could show Miss Val what skills I had. I first made a hamburger. This was after having a burger for lunch and being stuffed to the max. She said that I could have it, but I was way too full and politely refused. I made ceviche that impressed her so much that she made it for her friends for the Super Bowl weekend that year. Her class was fun. There was no pressure whatsoever in her class. It was laid back which I like. Near the end of my stay, I decided on making some chalupas. I would be using a gas burner stove. I just love the taste of a slightly-burned corn tortilla. Mmm. So, I'm frying the tortilla in hot oil and I can feel the heat from the flame. I have a paper plate with a paper towel on top, to soak up the excess grease. It's next to the stove. Then I start to smell something burning. *Oh, fuck!* I didn't say that, but thought it. The paper towel caught on fire and I knew it so I quickly grabbed it and put it in the sink which was right there to my left. I was feeling for the water faucet, when Miss Cisco was right there to turn it on! Whew! I'm glad that the fire alarm didn't go off as it was pretty cold in the 30's. Here, that's cold. People would have been a little irked by that. I knew that there was a big box of baking soda on the counter to use for such an occasion, next to the stove, but I didn't want to ruin my chalupa! And it was good! Miss Cisco thought so too.

In my Industrial Arts class, we learned how to replace a plain door knob, one with a lock and a deadbolt lock. We also learned how to fix a toilet and change out the parts and how to make a lamp, all while being blind-folded. Teacher Willie, Bill and Kelley were my teachers and they were all very cool. One of the younger kids Paul, was a riot. He was funny and kept us all entertained a bit. At least he kept it interesting. He was only twenty years old.

On one assignment in O&M, I told Miss Daisy that I would meet her at one of the bus stops. She had to put a letter in the mailbox; it was in the opposite direction. No problem, it was a straight shot. I just had to stay on the sidewalk. I start walking happy-go-lucky and I'm thinking, Shit, where's the driveway? All of a sudden a car passes me on the left. FUCK! I'm in the middle of the f'ing road! I quickly made my way to the sidewalk and had a good chuckle later. I'm pretty sure it scared Daisy a little. Whew!

One cold morning Daisy drove me to a park and made me climb a hill, blind-folded right. It was rather a little scary as I didn't want to fall off the side which was on both sides! I think that was the scariest time. Well, except for when I got my new hearing aids and I had to go to a busy intersection cross-walk on Lamar and Burnett. It was like I was right next to the cars. They were so loud and hauling ass within a few feet of me! I had to cross each intersection several times. A couple of times she had to shove me a bit so that I wouldn't bump into a car. I felt like Dustin Hoffman in "Midnight Cowboy," I'M WALKING OVA HEA! I did get to say it once! Another time I was supposed to go to the UT campus and find the bookstore. I'm at the crosswalk and I walk across the street or so I think, and I ask a woman, how far the bookstore was. I then ask her, where we were and she said the CO-OP. What? Shit! I did one of those banana things where I curved to the left and came back around behind the bus! The bus driver had honked AT ME! I thought that he was honking at someone else! She asked if she could walk me, but I said no, it's OK, just point me in the right direction. That was too funny.

Mike did my tech evaluation. He asked me to do several tasks on a computer. I did OK and typed forty-eight words a minute on my first try. My index finger is a little messed up on my right hand. I get my u's and y's, and my m's, n's, and b's mixed up. He was such a cool teacher. He's got a million things on his mind at any one time. I thought and was hoping that he was going to be my tech teacher. He was later on after a couple of months. Everyone liked him, especially the students. He now comes to my house when I need some tech assistance, like setting up my computer and all kinds of other stuff. He also works for iCanConnect. They are associated with the Helen Keller Foundation and they were able to get me a free iphone and a laptop computer with a docking station. How freaking cool was that. I had never, ever had a smart phone. Shit it was already 2019! I had no idea how to use one. I have since been upgraded to an iphone 13 and will soon be getting a new desktop! What wonderful people, I am so grateful.

Miss Sarah had moved to another department within CCRC. She was now with Deaf and Hard of Hearing. I had my IOS with her and she taught me how to use my new iphone. She was a very, very cool lady, so easy to talk with. I really felt like many of the people working there at CCRC were my "guardian angels" so to speak.

Once I completed my Industrial Arts course with the completion of my lamp, I had Career Counseling, which I was excited to begin. Let me just say, that I made that lamp blind-folded and from scratch. I had to measure and cut the wood, after deciding what kind of design I was going to have. I decide on two blocks one top of the other with the base being bigger. Then I had to sand it and then rub some bees wax on it for a little glow. Kelley then burned the outline of a Mandarin fish on the front of it. I was really proud of myself. I've grown up using all kinds of power tools so it was really fun for me.

In my Career Counseling class, my teacher Mrs. Brooks, Jennifer was a bundle of unbridled energy. When I first met her she was surprised to learn that I had taught at Hays High School, where she was a student. I left in 2004, the year she was a freshman. She was so excited and I even knew both of her parents! Shit, we were like feeding off of each other's energy. We were both very excited. I had to re-do my résumé and was ready to start so that I could start working. I wanted to start working again. I had never been out of work since I was twelve years old mowing lawns. It was an exciting time.

Towards the end of the course I started doing volunteer work at Casa Marianela, an immigrant shelter, helping teach ESL classes. I sat in on the beginning class at first and their little children roaming the house that we were having the class in. It was quite chaotic. Miss Marlene, the Director was a very cool lady as well. She knew all of the kids and adults names, and there were plenty! I really admired her for giving her "all" to the immigrants. She had lived in Spain sometime and spoke excellent Spanish. The immigrants were from all over Africa, Nigeria, Mali, The Democratic Republic of the Congo, Kenya and other countries. Many had gone through South America and up through Central America and Mexico. There were also Colombians, Brazilians, Venezuelan, etc. I enjoyed speaking Spanish with them and would often translate to help them understand better. Some had pretty good English speaking skills, while others were very rudimentary. It was quite enjoyable going. Another student, Marty, would go with me so that she could learn English. I would help her with English and wrote some phrases for her on how to say different things.

One weekend some of the younger people had gone to a concert at Stubb's there in Austin. They had gone to see the Dropkick Murphys. They all bought tickets and showed up with their white canes to the show. It was Ben, Helen, Shady and a couple of other people. Once inside the venue, some crew members had seen the "blind people" and gave them backstage passes, all access with all of the amenities, food! That was so cool of the band to do that. I wish more people were that considerate and mindful. I think it was Helen that said she overheard someone in crowd say, "Why do they get to go up to the stage, they can't even see!" Fran hadn't heard that, otherwise, he said that he would have gone at 'em. Blind people can still feel the excitement of just being there in the moment. It's too bad that there are so many mindless people in our country.

One of my O&M assignments was to take a Metro Access somewhere in North Austin. It could be anywhere, only had to be on this side of the river. One of my favorite places that I used to go and haven't been to in many years was Book People. It's an awesome book store. They have all kinds of cool artsy stuff too. I had a hard time walking out of that store without spending at least $75 on books! When I arrived, I checked in my backpack and put on my eSight glasses. My eyes watered as I looked at the first bookcase with new arrivals. It was so exciting. Yes, it was exciting for me to see all of those books and be able to read them. It still took a little work to get the glasses adjusted just right to get the maximum benefit. I stayed there only an hour as I had to get back to campus for lunch.

All of the cafeteria workers were very nice and tried to learn and call everyone by their names. Miss Sarita was a Panamanian woman who was almost like family. I told her that I had made some good ceviche and brought her some. She liked it too, but I don't think it was spicy enough for her taste. She told me that she would make some the following week for everyone. She did and it was very good and yes, it was spicier than mine. Everything they served was so good. They also had a salad bar that was excellent. I usually ate a salad if I knew that I would be cooking in class right after lunch. Once a month, on a Thursday the cafeteria staff would prepare a big meal with a couple of entrees buffet style. We would line up and serve ourselves. Sometimes it was difficult because you couldn't really see how much we were serving ourselves. It was very nice and they would put tablecloths on the tables and separate them as in a restaurant. I was always hungry. I needed to eat this much to have all the energy I needed to get me through my classes. It had jump-started my metabolism. With my family not being here with me, I almost felt guilty eating this good. It was three well-balanced meals every day. I can't remember when I used to eat that good. I mean, don't get me wrong, my wife cooks very well too, but not every single meal. I eat leftovers all the time and I don't mind that at all. I don't have to have something home-cooked for every meal!

    I did graduate in June of 2019. I went to an interview at the Prison Facility there in Lockhart for a job interview for a substitute teacher position. I did show up with my cane, and I thought the interview went well. I however, didn't get the job. I also had applied for another job with no success. In September, I decided to write a book about my adventures. It took me two years to finish. I was fortunate to get my manuscript accepted for publication. I started this book in September of 2021. My second book only took less than four months to write. I think that I may have one or possibly two more books left in me.

    To his credit, Mr. Jones, the Lockhart Superintendent did do a good job of keeping parents informed during the pandemic quarantine and lockdown. He communicated good information to the parents as soon as he knew something. It was unfortunate that the School Board had decided against mask mandates at the beginning of the 2021-2022 school year. Governor Abbott made sure to threaten districts if they had. We could not send our grand-daughters back to this district after that decision. I still strongly feel that Superintendent Jones did me wrong.

A CHICANO SPANISH TEACHER

We've had to face many obstacles as many families often do, especially after my retirement. Our landlord was increasing our rent "significantly" he said. I was already paying $1300 a month. He could definitely get more and should as taxes have gone up quite a bit. Lots of people are moving in to the smaller towns surrounding Austin. Lydia had mentioned this to her son Derek, who had an empty house in Kyle where he had been living. His children and our grandchildren, live with their mother in Buda. He had just gotten a new job in South Texas and would not be living there at all during the week. He had a big four bedroom two-story house that was empty and we would have to ourselves except when the kids would stay with us every other weekend. Problem solved. Thank you Lordy!

This was in early September when I had gotten my first manuscript approved for publication by three publishing companies. I was so surprised, but I have to admit, that it was a great ego booster, something I needed. To me, this was progress; all I needed was to find a way to pay for the services. We were in the process of moving. We had a lot of stuff, too much and had a yard sale. We practically gave away most of the stuff. In Lockhart, if you want to get rid of something, you can put it outside by the curb and someone will come by to pick it up. It doesn't take long at all. I had already started writing this book and I wanted to finish the Junior High and Last Assignment chapters since they both involved Lockhart. I wanted to be done by the end of September, when we would move to Kyle.

We made the move and we all are very happy here. It doesn't feel as oppressive as Lockhart had started to feel to us. I will miss my neighbor Zeke he was such a good person and friend. I will also miss most of all Mario's restaurant. Best tacos and food in Texas! Great people too! Kyle, I hope, will bring us more employment opportunities. Lockhart had few. I'm so lucky that I have Lydia, she really does take good care of me and the girls and kids. I'm hoping that the publication of my books and possibly books, will lead to more employment opportunities, we'll see.

It was a nice surprise to find out that Tony had partnered with another group to open a live music venue here in Kyle. It's called the Rail House. I'm so proud of him. It's nice to know that good things do happen to good people. I'm sure that by opening this venue he's made many people in this area very, very happy, starting with me.

Our grand-daughters are fully vaccinated and will begin in person school here in the Hays C.I.S.D. in Kyle. I know that they will be better suited for this district, I hope. Their first day of school begins tomorrow morning. They are both kind, smart, and curious which is a good recipe to have for learning to take place. I must also add that during our time in Lockhart when Veronica and Carol were five and six all the way until they were eleven and twelve, Lydia and I got to see all of the changes that they have gone through. One joke that Veronica made up when she was five was priceless. It goes like this. What did one poop ask the other poop? What did you do today?

As it turns out, we were to be in Kyle for only just over eight months before it would be time once again to move. The girls tried going to school but it didn't work out. Too many kids in school with CO-VID and no mask mandates. This would not work for us so it was back to online school. They were getting tired of it as well.

While going through our stuff, I decided to sell some amps and my PRS guitar to finish paying off my book. When I got my first copy there was an error that had to be corrected. It took rather long to exit the Corrections department. I finally got my corrected copy in late July. They will not be working on the distribution and promotion of the book. We were so busy getting ready for the move it was almost like a blessing for the delay. In the meantime, I would be working on my mailing list for the publisher.

This time we would be moving to Victoria, Texas, where our grand children's mother, Cree and her husband live. They are now eleven and twelve and have been out of school for just over two years and it's time to get them back into the school routine. They need to be with kids their own age and with live teachers. I know that the teaching profession is hurting right now with so many teachers retiring. I would

A CHICANO SPANISH TEACHER

not go back to teaching for anything! It's too much for me now; it gets harder and more difficult every year. We got the grand-children registered at the same Junior High School. They are both highly intelligent. They could read before Kindergarten. We've always told them that it does not matter to us who you like. They both have made friends and they said that many of their classmates can't even read!

Some of the teachers here at their school treat the kids differently. First, they punish all of the class for the misdeeds of one or two, Anglo teachers being short with non-white children. One Hispanic substitute teacher address one of my grand-daughter's black friends as, she was calling attendance and called out her two black friends names then said, your name is now little black girl and you are little ghetto black girl. Now, I know how children can speak in hyperbole, but our grandchildren don't even curse in front of us! She was walking down the hallway holding hands with a couple of friends, a boy and a girl. A teacher looked at her and said it wasn't okay for her to hold hands with the girl. It was ok with the boy! Can you tell that this is a conservative school district? Teacher treat boys differently than girls and some little assholes don't ever get disciplined. I'm trying my Lord, I'm trying!

The oldest of our grandchildren living with us has friends of all colors, black, white, and brown. Her black friends call her "whitechocolate." I think that's pretty cool. It has gotten so toxic at their school that we decided to withdraw them and go back to home schooling them. I wish they had better schools or at least schools where the teachers and students are held accountable for their actions or inactions. I refuse to put them through all of that! Its sad. I didn't want them to have to go back to home schooling, but what can we do? They really were enjoying school at first. Its just sad.

My file from the Texas Workforce Commission was to be mailed to the Victoria office so that they can assist me in finding a job. I never had to struggle before like I am now trying to stay afloat. The Child Tax Credit that we were receiving helped us out so much. When the Republicans and Sinema and Manchin took it away it hurt, and it hurt bad. It had helped out so many families. We know who is on the side of the people and who is on the side of the top 1 percent.

12. Onward Through the Fog

I lived most all of my life with excellent vision. I could hit a 95 mph fastball in my younger days. I was also a dead-shot with a rifle. I've seen so many things in my travels and in my scuba diving. I even went so far as to pick up underwater videography and photography. I have really been quite blessed and fortunate all through my life, so I can't really be too upset about my blind situation. It has been trying at times, but nevertheless seem to get past whatever obstacle may arise. I'm lucky to have a wife that makes all of my appointments by telephone to my various doctors, she has taken on much on my behalf, and also drives me to wherever I may need to go. She's been there for me and I can't say that enough! In this chapter I will be talking about my journey on this path. I have always believed that it is important to have a good sense of humor, and this sense of humor has gotten me through the fog along with my belief in the Divine. I have been fortunate to have had positive people on my path throughout my life, my family, friends, and teachers. My teachers at Criss Cole Rehabilitation Center for the Blind in Austin, Texas prepared me for this challenge. It was like spring training for going blind. I learned how to get around under my new condition. These are my stories.

On our way back home from a trip, Lydia and I were traveling coming in from Houston to Calallen. We would drive through Calallen on Hwy 326 heading west. When we came to the four-way stop, it was night and there were no other cars around. I started to turn left to go to Banquete, but I could not see the road even with the headlights turned on! Lydia then yelled, "Where are you going?" I yelled back, "I can't see the fucking road!" Shit! That was scary. She helped me with the steering wheel and managed to get on the right side of the road. I realized then that it would be difficult to continue driving at night.

On our drives to Corpus Christi I started noticing that it always seemed to be hazy. I would ask Lydia if it was hazy today, and often it was, but then not always. I also started to notice these "things" coming across my visual field. It almost looked like electrified DNA strands. They would float in all directions and change shapes. I decided to get me eyes checked so I went to an eye doctor in town and he prescribed me some glasses and also gave me some eye drops. One eye would all of a sudden get bloodshot. That was it. Wow! I could see much better! I kept seeing these "floaters" across my visual field and wanted to know what they were. I went to another doctor in town, but he couldn't tell me anything. After that, I ended up seeing two specialists in Corpus Christi with no better results. One of my old friends from the neighborhood was visiting and he told me of his eye doctor in Houston. He was describing some of the same symptoms that I had. He had surgery to have it corrected and could now see very well. I was hoping that would be the case for me as well. So, when I went to see his doctor, the doctor ran all kinds of tests on me and had me go to one of his colleague's office for a special test that he did not have the equipment for. We went and had the test done and returned to the doctor's office. He then tells me that I have Retinitis Pigmentosa, or more precisely hereditary photoreceptor dystrophy, and you're going blind. Finally! I know what I have. I was happy, really, I was. My wife was crying and my mother looked worried. I was just glad that I finally knew what I had. The "floaters" are undissolved gel-like particles that pass across the retina or something. That was in 2015, now in 2022 those "floaters" are still around but had turned neon-green instead of the electric look that it had before. When I sneeze or cough, they come out in abundance and I'm even more blinded. I still had a year and a half to teach and it was horrible as earlier mentioned. It was so difficult trying to learn the students' names because I had so many of them. My lack of vision did not help the situation. On the last day of school June 2, 2017 I parked the car and never drove again. It was far too dangerous by this time.

I had a very large corner lot to maintain. It was quite large. I use a push mower to do the whole enchilada. I would go around picking up whatever I could find in the yard before mowing. Nevertheless, I still managed to destroy scuba masks, garden hoses, flip-flops, soccer balls, floats, a large patio umbrella the pole and the shade, a weed-eater, a sewage pipe at my neighbor's back of the fence; I wanted to stay busy and offered to do his yard, he's done mine also. That one bent the blade real good. Lydia got me a new one at Ace Hardware. One morning as there was no one at home, the bedroom door was open halfway and I could not see it and hit the door with all of my weight and it did not budge a bit. I freaking saw stars amigo! I also got a bloody nose! Lydia came in shortly and I had to explain what had happened. Only recently I was weed-eating along the fence at our new place in Victoria, and as I was trying to hit the kill switch and not paying attention I ran face-first into the palm tree in the back yard. It was overcast and just blended in. It's always at the "last second" that I see shit. Again, I got a bloody freaking nose. I went to one knee; I saw stars again. As soon as I wondered if my nose was going to bleed, it did. I was up with the water hose and let Lydia know of yet another "mishap." This one takes the prize. When I was in Lockhart taking care of my backyard, as I was walking by the trampoline, I ran my hand by the bottom of the frame that was about waist high. As I did this, I felt what I thought was the fluffy tops of weeds. As I passed by, I thought that I would pull them on my way back. When I came back to the trampoline, I felt for the "weeds." All I feel is freaking electric-fire! The little fluffy weeds were actually yellow-jackets wings. They must have been stunned when I first touch them and let it "slide." Not this time baby! I sprang back quickly as soon as I realized what was happening. I ran into the house and was screaming. I was on the dining room floor screaming and scaring the kids. Veronica later told me that she walked in but didn't know how to respond so she went back into her room. The wasps had stung me in five places on my hand, on my elbow, shoulder and head.

I was mowing in the front yard of our place in Victoria. There is a huge Crepe Myrtle tree on the side of the house. As I was mowing by the tree, there was a wasp's nest on a low hanging branch. Of course, I did not see it but felt the stings immediately. I got stung eight times! Three on my back, one on my shoulder, two on the back of my head and two more on my arms. Good thing I'm not allergic!

I see light and dark shapes. I don't see color too much at all and my depth perception is non-existent. It's much easier to see a computer screen with reverse contrast, but the fog is still getting thicker.

Right now, is a good time for our leaders to change up our educational system. Not all students go or need to go to college, but everyone needs a job. Companies need to provide more apprenticeships and internships to help with this need. By the time students are in fifth or sixth grade, they would be headed for a higher education or main-lined into the workforce. I don't have all of the answers, but what I do know is that teachers want to teach without the distractions that disruptive kids bring to the classroom. It's so hard to be a teacher these days.

I wish you a happy 2023! Let's all work together for the benefit of the entire world, with a message of Peace and Goodwill to All. Let's all try to smile a little more!

13. Acknowledgements:

I would like to thank all of my teachers not just in education but in life, like my grandparents, family, teachers, coaches, neighbors and friends, my brother Adrian, my best friends Jimmy Soliz and Jerry Hallstrom, Rest in Peace my brothers, Louie Garza, Randy Hashem, and many more. My typing teacher Mrs. Dietrich for her patience and for teaching me the skill I would use for the rest of my life. Coach Carrillo for showing me how to be a leader and believe in myself while teaching me to be a quarterback. I'd also like to thank my excellent professors like Dr. Charles Richard Carlisle and Dr. James Champion for being the main inspiration for me in becoming a teacher. I want to thank the excellent co-workers I had the pleasure to know and work with like Dr. Javier Villarreal, Joyce Sommerfield, Debbie Lefevre, Mike Snodgrass, Mr. & Mrs. David Pringles, Diane Berry Koenig, Terry Fraley, my Last Frontier mentor, Karen Zepeda, all those who I shared music with like Rosie Mora, I am lucky and proud to call Miss Gracie Peña who became a Spanish teacher despite having many obstacles and who became a friend and trusted confidant, I love you girl, all of my bandmates, both student and faculty throughout the years especially Anthony Stevenson, Bradley Hamilton, Noel Estrada, Sonny Garcia and Ryan Cassidy. I also want to thank Miranda Beard, my former student who would become my step-daughter who showed me a picture of her mother that would be the ticket to the rollercoaster ride of my life. I enjoyed the laughter and humor that the students and I shared in class; and to all of the wonderful students that I had in every school that I taught. I pray for those students who were troubled and wish them all peace and prosperity in their futures.

SONNY MORIN

Important Message to All Texas Teachers:

    Teachers when you are getting close to retirement, please start to put some money into Social Security. I have always had good health throughout my years. However, as we age, shit starts happening. I retired at age 56 with my vision deteriorating. I tried to apply for Social Security Disability, but was denied because I had not contributed to Social Security in my last four quarters is what they told me. I was several credits short. I had contributed to SS in the middle of my career, but when I changed schools, I did not continue with that. Then I thought that I could possibly get SS early at age 62. Well, I got denied that as well and for the same reason. Let me tell you it's been a struggle, so please Teachers of Texas start putting some $ into Social Security. I know I'll find a job soon! Amen.

www.ingramcontent.com/pod-product-compliance
Lightning Source LLC
Chambersburg PA
CBHW020310010526
44107CB00001B/51